1000 FACTS ABOUT THE UNITED STATES OF AMERICA VOL. 2

Contents

3

"Where liberty dwells, there is my country."

— Benjamin Franklin

Introduction

Welcome to the second installment of the "1000 Facts about The United States of America" series. This trilogy is designed as a deep dive into the heart and soul of one of the world's most fascinating countries. With the first volume, we embarked on a captivating journey, unearthing hidden gems of information about the United States and its unique states. This second volume continues that journey, offering even more exciting discoveries about this diverse and dynamic nation.

America's story is not monolithic; it's a patchwork quilt of histories, cultures, experiences, and landscapes. This volume explores this rich tapestry further, delving deeper into each state's unique narrative. The facts encapsulated within these pages span across various domains such as history, geography, culture, economy, politics, and many more, offering a multifaceted view of the country's vibrant and varied states.

From scientific breakthroughs that changed the world to small-town traditions that continue to enrich the nation's cultural landscape, this volume sheds light on the broad spectrum of experiences that define the American way of life. It is designed to educate, entertain, and inspire, revealing the hidden corners and unseen vistas of the United States, enhancing your understanding of this great nation.

Whether you're a trivia enthusiast, a history buff, or someone with an insatiable curiosity about the world, "1000 Facts about The United States of America vol. 2" offers a treasure trove of knowledge waiting to be discovered. Let's turn the page and continue our exploration of America's vast tapestry, revealing more of its intricate patterns and vibrant colors. Journey with us through these thousand facts, and deepen your appreciation of the United States' rich heritage and dynamic future.

Daniel Scott

Alabama

- **Civil Rights Landmarks:** Birmingham's Civil Rights District has been named a National Monument, commemorating pivotal events in the Civil Rights Movement.
- **Snake Church:** A small sect in Alabama practices a religious ceremony that involves handling venomous snakes.
- **Legendary Trail:** The Selma to Montgomery National Historic Trail traces the 54-mile route civil rights activists marched in 1965.
- **Cahaba Lilies:** The Cahaba River in Alabama is one of the few places in the world you can see the stunning Cahaba lilies bloom in the wild.
- **Aquatic Richness:** Alabama has more species of freshwater fish, mussels, snails, turtles, and crayfish than any other state.
- **Vineyard Surprise:** Alabama is home to the southernmost vineyard in the United States, Perdido Vineyards.
- **Steel City:** Birmingham was once the primary industrial center of the Southern U.S. and was nicknamed the "Pittsburgh of the South."
- **Famed Tuskegee Airmen:** The Tuskegee Airmen, the first African American military aviators, trained in Tuskegee, Alabama.
- **Appalachian Beginnings:** Alabama marks the southern end of the Appalachian Mountains and the famous Appalachian Trail.
- **Covered Bridges:** Alabama is home to 11 historic covered bridges still standing today.
- **Watercress Capital:** Huntsville is known as the watercress capital of the world.
- **Big Bob Gibson:** Decatur, Alabama, is the birthplace of the white barbecue sauce, a mayonnaise-based concoction created by Big Bob Gibson Bar-B-Q.
- **Legendary Amphibian:** The Red Hills salamander, Alabama's state amphibian, is found nowhere else in the world.

- **Conecuh Sausage:** Evergreen, Alabama, is the home of the famed Conecuh sausage, a regional culinary favorite.
- **Oyster Farming:** Alabama is a leading state in oyster aquaculture, known for its "off-bottom" farming technique.
- **Preservation of History:** Mobile, Alabama, is home to the Battleship Memorial Park, where the historic USS Alabama is docked.
- **Gulf Coast Beaches:** Alabama has 32 miles of white-sand beaches along the Gulf of Mexico.
- **Rocket Center:** The U.S. Space & Rocket Center in Huntsville is home to Space Camp, inspiring young astronauts since 1982.
- **Golfers' Paradise:** Alabama's Robert Trent Jones Golf Trail is the largest golf course construction project ever attempted, with 468 holes at 11 sites across the state.
- **Largest Cast-Iron Statue:** Birmingham's Vulcan statue is the world's largest cast-iron statue and reflects the city's roots in the iron and steel industry.

Alaska

- **Time Zone Rarity:** Alaska has its own time zone, the Alaska Standard Time.
- **Walrus Islands:** Alaska's Walrus Islands are the largest terrestrial haulout for Pacific walrus in North America.
- **Floating Post Office:** Douglas Island hosts the "Mail Boat Run," the last floating post office in the U.S.
- **Yukon River:** The 3rd longest river in the U.S., the Yukon River, runs through Alaska and has played a significant role in the state's history and economy.
- **Mosquito Reputation:** In some parts of Alaska, mosquitoes are jokingly referred to as the state bird due to their large size and abundant presence.
- **Birdwatchers' Paradise:** The Alaska Maritime National Wildlife Refuge is home to 40 million seabirds, representing 80% of North American seabirds.
- **Whale Festivals:** The city of Sitka hosts an annual WhaleFest, celebrating the marine life in the surrounding waters.
- **Santa's Home:** The city of North Pole, Alaska, celebrates Christmas year-round, complete with candy cane street lights.
- **Ice Age Remnants:** Bering Land Bridge National Preserve in Alaska is a remnant of the land bridge that once connected Asia with North America over 13,000 years ago.
- **Largest National Forest:** The Tongass National Forest in Alaska is the largest national forest in the U.S.
- **Marine Highway:** The Alaska Marine Highway System, stretching 3,500 miles and serving 35 communities, is a unique mode of transportation in the state.
- **King Crab Hunting:** The Bering Sea off the coast of Alaska is known for its dangerous but lucrative king crab fishery, popularized by the TV show "Deadliest Catch."

- **Alaskan Bush Pilots:** Airplanes are a common mode of transportation in Alaska, leading to a high number of pilots per capita.
- **Sourdough Tradition:** Sourdough pancakes are a beloved breakfast staple in Alaska, a tradition dating back to the Klondike Gold Rush.
- **Alyeska Pipeline:** Alyeska Pipeline Service Company employs many Alaskans, managing the 800-mile Trans-Alaska Pipeline.
- **Russian Influence:** The Russian Orthodox Church remains a significant religious institution in Alaska, a testament to the state's Russian history.
- **Totem Poles:** Alaska has the world's largest collection of totem poles, a traditional form of Indigenous Alaskan art.
- **Juneau Access:** The capital of Alaska, Juneau, is only accessible by boat or plane, as no roads connect the city to the rest of Alaska.
- **Tiny Town:** Kupreanof, Alaska, with a population of just about 20 people, is one of the smallest towns in the U.S.
- **Little Diomede Island:** Little Diomede Island, Alaska, is just 2.4 miles away from Russia's Big Diomede Island, offering one of the closest points between the U.S. and Russia.

Arizona

- **Mt. Humphreys:** The highest point in Arizona, Humphreys Peak, stands at 12,633 feet above sea level.
- **Bat Caves:** Arizona's Kartchner Caverns State Park has one of the world's longest stalactite formations and houses about 1,000 bats.
- **Route 66:** The historic Route 66, a symbol of classic American culture, runs through Arizona.
- **Population Growth:** Arizona has been one of the fastest-growing states in terms of population.
- **Champagne Springs:** Arizona has a spring that emits pure carbon dioxide, giving the illusion of champagne bubbles.
- **Biosphere 2:** Arizona's Biosphere 2 is the world's largest science experiment, aiming to better understand Earth's systems.
- **World Oldest Rodeo:** The city of Prescott, Arizona, has been hosting the "World's Oldest Rodeo" since 1888.
- **Skiing in the Desert:** Despite its desert landscape, Arizona has a ski resort, the Arizona Snowbowl.
- **Gem Shows:** The Tucson Gem, Mineral & Fossil Showcase is one of the most important gem and mineral shows worldwide.
- **Pima Air & Space Museum:** This museum in Tucson is one of the world's largest non-government-funded aerospace museums.
- **Famous Residents:** Notable people from Arizona include Cesar Chavez, Linda Ronstadt, and Sandra Day O'Connor, the first woman appointed to the U.S. Supreme Court.
- **Bird Diversity:** Arizona has a greater variety of birds than any other area of equal size in the U.S.
- **Kitt Peak Observatory:** Located on Kitt Peak of the Quinlan Mountains, it is the largest, most diverse gathering of astronomical instruments in the world.
- **National Monuments:** Arizona has more national monuments than any other state in the U.S.

- **Painted Desert:** This beautiful landscape features colorful stratified layers of siltstone, mudstone, and shale.
- **Arizona Diamondbacks:** In 2001, the Diamondbacks became the youngest expansion franchise in MLB history to win the World Series.
- **Arizona Highways Magazine:** Published since 1925, this award-winning magazine highlights travel, culture, and geography of the state.
- **Ghost Towns:** Arizona has over 275 ghost towns, remnants of mining boom towns of the late 19th and early 20th century.
- **Barry Goldwater:** The influential conservative U.S. Senator who ran for president in 1964 was from Arizona.
- **Besh-Ba-Gowah:** The ruins of an ancient Salado masonry pueblo are preserved at Besh-Ba-Gowah Archaeological Park in Globe, Arizona.

Arkansas

- **African American History:** Little Rock Central High School National Historic Site represents the struggle and eventual success of desegregation in America's schools.
- **Famous Bridges:** The Big River Crossing is the longest pedestrian and bicycle bridge in America crossing the Mississippi River.
- **Arkansas River:** One of the major rivers of the United States, it generally flows to the east and southeast, spanning over 1,469 miles.
- **Ozark National Forest:** This forest spans 1.2 million acres and includes over 500 species of trees and woody plants.
- **Crystal Bridges Museum:** Founded by Alice Walton, the heir to the Walmart fortune, this museum houses American masterpieces from the colonial era to contemporary work.
- **Famous Actors:** Billy Bob Thornton, a renowned actor, filmmaker, and musician was born in Hot Springs, Arkansas.
- **Rice Production:** Arkansas leads the U.S. in rice production, providing about half of the country's supply.
- **King Biscuit Blues Festival:** One of the nation's foremost showcases of blues music, held annually in Helena-West Helena.
- **Poet Laureate:** John Gould Fletcher, born in Little Rock, was the first Southern poet to win the Pulitzer Prize for Poetry.
- **Blanchard Springs Caverns:** This living cave, meaning it's still in the process of formation, is toured by thousands of visitors yearly.
- **Quartz Crystals:** Mount Ida area is referred to as the Quartz Crystal Capital of the World for its many quartz crystal formations.
- **World Championship Duck Calling Contest:** Held annually in Stuttgart, this competition attracts contestants from all over the U.S. and several foreign countries.
- **Wildlife Diversity:** Arkansas is home to over 300 species of birds, 60 mammals, 93 reptiles and amphibians, and more than 200 fish species.

- **Eureka Springs:** This entire Victorian-era town is listed on the National Register of Historic Places.
- **Famous TV Producer:** Television producer and writer Douglas Heyes, known for "The Twilight Zone," was born in Arkansas.
- **Arkansas Razorbacks:** The University of Arkansas' football team is named after the feral pig, a symbol of tenacity and fearlessness.
- **Buffalo National River:** Established in 1972, this was America's first national river, known for its unpolluted water and spectacular bluffs.
- **State Drink:** Arkansas declared milk as its official state beverage in 1985, promoting the dairy industry.
- **Village Creek State Park:** This park spans almost 7,000 acres and includes a unique geologic feature: Crowley's Ridge.
- **Historic State Parks:** Arkansas's state park system is one of the oldest and most distinguished in the United States.

California

- **Surfing Capital:** Huntington Beach is known as "Surf City," hosting world-famous surfing competitions annually.
- **In-N-Out Burger:** This popular fast-food chain, beloved for its "Animal Style" burgers and fries, was founded in Baldwin Park in 1948.
- **San Francisco Cable Cars:** The world's last manually operated cable car system is an icon of San Francisco.
- **Catalina Island:** Just off the coast, this island paradise offers pristine beaches and abundant wildlife.
- **San Andreas Fault:** This major fault line cutting across California is responsible for the state's frequent earthquakes.
- **The Zamboni:** The ice resurfacer used in ice rinks around the world was invented by Frank J. Zamboni in Paramount, California.
- **State Animal:** The California grizzly bear, featured on the state flag, is the official state animal.
- **L.A.'s Olvera Street:** Known as "the birthplace of Los Angeles," Olvera Street is part of the El Pueblo de Los Angeles Historic Monument.
- **The Getty Center:** In Los Angeles, this museum is renowned for its collection of European paintings, sculpture, and decorative arts.
- **Salton Sea:** This is the largest lake in California, formed by a flood in 1905 in which the Colorado River flowed into the Salton Sink for two years.
- **Fresno Raisins:** Over half of the raisins in the U.S. come from around Fresno, thanks to the city's perfect grape-growing climate.
- **First Motion Picture Theater:** The world's first permanent motion picture theater, the "Nickelodeon," opened in Los Angeles on June 19, 1905.

- **Largest County:** San Bernardino County is the largest county in the U.S., spanning over 20,000 square miles.
- **Jelly Belly:** The Jelly Belly Candy Company, known for its jelly beans in many flavors, is based in Fairfield, California.
- **Ski and Surf in One Day:** The state's unique geography allows you to surf in the morning and ski in the afternoon.
- **Nobel Laureates:** The University of California system boasts more than 60 Nobel laureates, underscoring the state's academic excellence.
- **Chinatown Gates:** San Francisco's Chinatown, the oldest in North America, is famous for its iconic Dragon Gate.
- **Ghost Towns:** Due to the Gold Rush era, California is home to numerous ghost towns that are remnants of a bygone age.
- **Spanish Missions:** The 21 Spanish missions in California, established between 1769 and 1823, played a crucial role in the state's history.
- **Santa Ana Winds:** These strong, extremely dry downslope winds significantly affect California's weather and are a key factor in wildfires.

Colorado

- **The Stanley Hotel:** Located in Estes Park, this hotel was the inspiration for Stephen King's "The Shining."
- **Fort Collins:** Known for its historic downtown, Colorado State University, and a number of craft breweries.
- **Olympic Training Center:** Located in Colorado Springs, it's the flagship training center for the U.S. Olympic Committee and the home of U.S. Paralympics.
- **Colorado Gold Rush:** Prompted by the discovery of gold in the 1850s, it brought a large influx of settlers to the state.
- **Telluride Film Festival:** An annual film festival that attracts top filmmakers and celebrities to the small mountain town.
- **Mount Elbert:** The highest peak in Colorado, and the second highest in the contiguous U.S., standing at 14,439 feet above sea level.
- **Denver Art Museum:** One of the largest art museums between the West Coast and Chicago, it's known for its collection of American Indian art.
- **Black Canyon of the Gunnison:** Known for its steep cliffs, older than the Grand Canyon, and craggy spires.
- **UFO Watchtower:** Located in Hooper, it's a unique roadside attraction for those interested in extraterrestrial life.
- **Chimney Rock National Monument:** This archeological site was home to the ancestors of the modern Pueblo Indians 1,000 years ago.
- **Colorado Trail:** Stretching for 500 miles from Denver to Durango, it passes through some of the most spectacular scenery in the Rockies.
- **Casa Bonita:** Made famous by an episode of South Park, this Mexican restaurant in Denver features cliff divers and a unique dining experience.

- **Largest Natural Hot Springs Pool:** Located in Glenwood Springs, it has been a haven for those seeking wellness for over a century.
- **Fittest State:** Colorado often ranks as the fittest state in the U.S., with the lowest rates of obesity.
- **The Wild Animal Sanctuary:** Located in Keenesburg, it's the largest nonprofit carnivore sanctuary in the world, spanning 789 acres.
- **Colorado Day:** Celebrated on the 1st of August, it commemorates the day Colorado was admitted to the Union in 1876.
- **Blue Mustang:** Also known as Blucifer, it's a 32-foot tall fiberglass sculpture of a horse located at Denver International Airport.
- **Cripple Creek:** Once a gold mining camp, it's now a popular tourist spot with legal casinos and Victorian architecture.
- **Colorado State Fair:** Held annually in Pueblo since 1872, it offers fun events such as rodeos, concerts, and agricultural exhibits.
- **NORAD Headquarters:** Located in Cheyenne Mountain, it's a central hub for defense against missile attacks and space surveillance.

Connecticut

- **P.T. Barnum:** The famous showman and founder of the Barnum & Bailey Circus was born in Bethel, Connecticut.
- **USS Nautilus:** The world's first nuclear-powered submarine, it's now a museum ship in Groton.
- **Hartford's Insurance Industry:** Known as the "Insurance Capital of the World," Hartford is home to many insurance company headquarters.
- **First Lollipop:** The modern style of lollipop was first made in New Haven by the Bradley Smith Company in 1908.
- **Nathan Hale Homestead:** The childhood home of Connecticut's state hero, who was a spy during the American Revolution.
- **New Haven Green:** One of the oldest and most well-known town greens in the nation, dating back to the 1600s.
- **Old Newgate Prison:** Originally a copper mine, it was turned into a prison in the 18th century and is now a museum.
- **Ivoryton:** The small village was once the center of the world's ivory industry, with over half the world's ivory combs made there in the 19th century.
- **Griswold v. Connecticut:** This landmark 1965 Supreme Court case, originating in Connecticut, led to the legalization of birth control in the U.S.
- **Gungywamp:** An archaeological site in Groton featuring Colonial and Native American artifacts, along with mysterious stone structures.
- **Coltsville National Historical Park:** This park in Hartford preserves the site of Samuel Colt's firearms manufacturing facility.
- **University of Connecticut:** Known for its strong basketball programs, it's the largest public university in New England.
- **Lobster Rolls:** Connecticut-style lobster rolls are distinct, served warm and buttered rather than cold with mayo.

- **Steamed Cheeseburgers:** A regional specialty, these burgers are cooked in a steam cabinet and often served with melted cheese and onions.
- **Thimble Islands:** An archipelago in Long Island Sound, some of these tiny islands have just one house on them.
- **White Memorial Conservation Center:** Covering over 4,000 acres, it's Connecticut's largest nature center and wildlife sanctuary.
- **First Speed Limit Laws:** The first laws to restrict the speed of motor vehicles were enacted in Connecticut in 1901.
- **Connecticut Wine Trail:** Features 25 wineries and vineyards, showcasing the state's growing wine industry.
- **First Public Art Museum:** The Wadsworth Atheneum in Hartford was the first public art museum in the U.S.
- **Saville Dam:** An architectural marvel in Barkhamsted, the dam creates the Barkhamsted Reservoir, supplying water to Hartford.

Delaware

- **Delaware Agricultural Museum and Village:** Showcases the state's farming history with a collection of antique farm equipment and historical buildings.
- **Bombay Hook National Wildlife Refuge:** A crucial stopover for migrating birds, its tidal salt marshes attract hundreds of thousands of waterfowl each year.
- **Cape Henlopen State Park:** This beautiful coastal park features a WWII observation tower that offers panoramic views of the coast.
- **Wilmington and Western Railroad:** A heritage railroad offering steam- and diesel-powered rides through the scenic Red Clay Valley.
- **First State National Historical Park:** Delaware's only National Park, it celebrates the cultural and natural history of the first state.
- **Delaware Art Museum:** Known for its collection of British Pre-Raphaelite art, American art, and illustrations.
- **New Castle Courthouse:** Built in 1732, it's one of the oldest surviving courthouses in the U.S. and was Delaware's first state capitol.
- **Brandywine Creek:** This beautiful waterway played a significant role in early industrial America and was the scene of a major Revolutionary War battle.
- **Fenwick Island Lighthouse:** Standing since 1859, it's a major landmark and navigation aid at the Delaware/Maryland border.
- **Seaford:** The "Nylon Capital of the World," Seaford was home to the first nylon plant in the DuPont company.
- **Zwaanendael Museum:** Built to honor the 300th anniversary of the first European colony in Delaware, it now showcases the state's maritime, military, and social history.

- **Nanticoke Indian Tribe:** One of the oldest indigenous groups in the U.S., the Nanticoke people are a vibrant part of Delaware's cultural heritage.
- **Delaware State Fair:** Held annually in Harrington, it's a ten-day event featuring concerts, competitive exhibits, a carnival, and more.
- **Blue Hen Chicken:** The official state bird, it's an American breed of chicken that was a popular bird for cockfighting during Revolutionary War times.
- **Dewey Beach:** Known for its vibrant nightlife and popular live music scene.
- **Christina River:** A major river in the state, it was historically important for commerce and transportation.
- **Dogfish Head Brewery:** One of the best-known craft breweries in the U.S., based in Milton.
- **Delaware State University:** A historically black university, it's known for its programs in education, business, and applied sciences.
- **Delaware State Parks:** Despite its small size, Delaware has 16 state parks that offer a range of recreational opportunities.
- **Pea Patch Island:** This island in the Delaware River is home to Fort Delaware and one of the largest heronries on the East Coast.

Florida

- **Florida's Beaches:** Florida boasts more than 1,300 miles of coastline, more than any other state in the contiguous U.S.
- **Calle Ocho Festival:** The largest Hispanic festival in the U.S., held annually in Miami's Little Havana neighborhood.
- **Sawgrass Mills:** Located in Sunrise, it's one of the largest outlet and value retail shopping destinations in the U.S.
- **Ringling Bros. and Barnum & Bailey Circus:** Once had its winter headquarters in Sarasota, Florida.
- **Gatorland:** A 110-acre theme park and wildlife preserve in Orlando, known as the "Alligator Capital of the World."
- **Marjory Stoneman Douglas House:** The home of the journalist and environmentalist who wrote "The Everglades: River of Grass."
- **Florida's Population:** As of my knowledge cut-off in September 2021, Florida is the third most populous state in the U.S.
- **Homestead Miami Speedway:** A motor racing track located in Homestead, frequently hosting NASCAR and other major racing events.
- **Miami's Cuban Influence:** Miami is home to the largest Cuban-American population in the U.S.
- **Salvador Dali Museum:** Located in St. Petersburg, it houses the largest collection of Dalí's works outside Europe.
- **Florida State Seminoles:** The athletic teams representing Florida State University, known for their successful football program.
- **St. Johns River:** One of the few rivers in the U.S. that flows north, a significant recreation destination in northern Florida.
- **The Breakers Palm Beach:** A historic hotel in Palm Beach, Florida, first opened in 1896, known for its opulent design.
- **Fort Lauderdale's Canals:** Fort Lauderdale is known as the "Venice of America" due to its expansive and intricate canal system.

- **Orange Blossom Special:** A deluxe passenger train on the Seaboard Air Line Railroad, named after Florida's official state flower.
- **Tampa Bay Buccaneers:** The NFL team based in Tampa, winners of Super Bowl XXXVII and Super Bowl LV.
- **Coral Castle:** A limestone structure created by the Latvian-American eccentric Edward Leedskalnin, located in Homestead.
- **Jacksonville:** The largest city by area in the contiguous U.S., located in northeastern Florida.
- **Clearwater Marine Aquarium:** Known for its resident dolphin, Winter, whose story inspired the film "Dolphin Tale."
- **Miami Dolphins:** The oldest professional sports team in Florida, they're the first (and so far only) team to complete a perfect season, including winning the Super Bowl.

Georgia

- **Georgia Dome:** Before its demolition in 2017, it was one of the largest domed structures in the world, hosting numerous sport events including two Super Bowls.
- **Lake Lanier:** A reservoir created by the completion of Buford Dam on the Chattahoochee River in 1956.
- **Chick-fil-A:** This fast food chain, famous for its chicken sandwiches, was founded in the Atlanta suburb of Hapeville in 1946.
- **The Walking Dead:** The popular television series has been filmed in various locations throughout Georgia.
- **Waffle House:** This restaurant chain, known for its round-the-clock diner-style service, was founded in Avondale Estates, a suburb of Atlanta.
- **Rock City Gardens:** A tourist attraction on Lookout Mountain that features rock formations and panoramic views.
- **Centers for Disease Control and Prevention (CDC):** This national public health institute is headquartered in Atlanta.
- **Margaret Mitchell:** The author of "Gone With the Wind" was born in Atlanta in 1900.
- **Atlanta Falcons:** The city's National Football League team, founded in 1965.
- **James Oglethorpe:** The founder of the Province of Georgia, the last of the Thirteen Colonies, in 1733.
- **Kennesaw Mountain National Battlefield Park:** An important Civil War site, preserving a battlefield from the Atlanta Campaign of 1864.
- **Midnight in the Garden of Good and Evil:** This best-selling book is set in and around Savannah.
- **Tabby Concrete:** A type of building material made from oyster-shell lime, sand, and whole oyster shells, common in coastal Georgia.

- **Georgia's Antebellum Trail:** A 100-mile trek through seven historic communities that escaped Sherman's burning march through Georgia.
- **Jimmy Carter:** The 39th U.S. president was born in Plains, Georgia, in 1924.
- **Atlanta Motor Speedway:** This premier NASCAR race track in Hampton has a seating capacity of 111,000.
- **Cumberland Island National Seashore:** The largest of Georgia's Golden Isles, known for its wild horses.
- **Gone with the Wind Museum:** Located in Marietta, it offers an extensive collection of memorabilia related to the famous film.
- **Prohibition of Alcohol:** Georgia was the first U.S. state to outlaw alcohol, in 1907, well before nationwide prohibition.
- **The Fox Theatre:** This iconic performing arts venue in Atlanta was originally planned as a large, opulent movie theater.

Hawaii

- **Hawaii Volcanoes National Park:** The park encompasses two active volcanoes: Kilauea, one of the world's most active volcanoes, and Mauna Loa, the world's most massive shield volcano.
- **Pineapple Production:** At one point, Hawaii supplied 80% of the world's canned pineapple.
- **Hawaiian Luau:** This traditional Hawaiian party or feast often features entertainment like hula and fire dancing.
- **Hawaiian Lei:** These flower garlands represent the aloha spirit and are used in ceremonies and celebrations.
- **Diamond Head:** This volcanic tuff cone on Oahu is a defining feature of the view known to residents and tourists of Waikiki.
- **Polynesian Cultural Center:** Located in Laie on the northern shore of Oahu, this popular tourist attraction includes a recreated village showcasing Polynesian culture.
- **Banzai Pipeline:** Known for its surf break, it's a popular spot for surf competitions due to its large waves.
- **Lanai Island:** Once known for its pineapple plantations, the island is now famous for its two high-caliber golf courses.
- **Na Pali Coast:** This state park on Kauai is known for its towering sea cliffs, narrow valleys, and cascading waterfalls.
- **Aloha Tower:** Once the tallest building in the islands, this Honolulu lighthouse is a welcoming beacon for cruise ships.
- **State Mammal:** The Hawaiian Hoary Bat is the official state land mammal, while the Humpback Whale is the state marine mammal.
- **Ukulele:** This musical instrument plays a central role in Hawaiian music and culture.
- **Waimea Canyon:** Often referred to as the "Grand Canyon of the Pacific," this canyon on Kauai is approximately ten miles long and up to 3,000 feet deep.

- **Molokai's Sea Cliffs:** The island of Molokai boasts the highest sea cliffs in the world, reaching heights of 3,900 feet.
- **Hanauma Bay:** Known for its abundant marine life, this bay on Oahu is a popular snorkeling spot.
- **State Dance:** The hula, performed either sitting (noho dance) or standing (luna dance), is the official state dance.
- **Road to Hana:** This popular tourist drive on Maui offers breathtaking ocean views and waterfalls.
- **Hawaiian Honeycreepers:** These unique bird species, which display an incredible range of beak shapes and sizes, evolved from a single ancestral species in the islands.
- **Hawaii's Coral Reefs:** The state's coral reefs are some of the most isolated in the world, supporting thousands of species of fish, invertebrates, and algae.
- **Black Sand Beaches:** Many of Hawaii's beaches, such as Punalu'u Beach on the Big Island, have black sand created by the rapid cooling of volcanic lava.

Idaho

- **Mountain Bluebird:** The state bird is the Mountain Bluebird, known for its beautiful, vibrant color.
- **Star Garnet:** Found in only two places in the world, the Star Garnet is the state gem.
- **Idaho Spud Bar:** This candy bar, popular since 1918, is shaped like a potato and made with a marshmallow center coated in chocolate.
- **Largest Wilderness:** The Frank Church-River of No Return Wilderness is the largest contiguous federally managed wilderness in the continental United States.
- **The Oregon Trail:** Idaho was part of the historic Oregon Trail, with many landmarks still visible today.
- **Huckleberry State Fruit:** The huckleberry, a small, sweet berry, is the official state fruit.
- **State Raptor:** The Peregrine Falcon is the state raptor, reflecting Idaho's commitment to protecting birds of prey.
- **Coeur d'Alene Resort:** The floating green at the resort's golf course is a one-of-a-kind engineering marvel.
- **Hemingway Memorial:** Located near Sun Valley, the memorial honors the famous author who spent his last years in Idaho.
- **Idaho Statehouse:** Known as the "Capitol of Light," the statehouse in Boise is heated geothermally.
- **Historic Prisons:** The Old Idaho Penitentiary, in operation from 1872 to 1973, is now a museum.
- **Bruneau Sand Dunes:** Home to the tallest single-structured sand dune in North America, rising 470 feet above the surrounding desert floor.
- **Silverwood Theme Park:** The largest theme and water park in the Northwest is located in Idaho.
- **Idaho State University:** Known for its health science programs and houses the Idaho College of Osteopathic Medicine.

- **Moon Landscape:** The moon-like landscape of Craters of the Moon National Monument was used by Apollo 14 astronauts for training.
- **The Sawtooth Mountains:** Named for their jagged peaks, the mountains are part of the Rocky Mountains and offer ample outdoor recreation opportunities.
- **Snake River:** The longest river in the state is known for its excellent fishing and whitewater rafting.
- **Cataldo Mission:** The oldest building in the state, also known as the Mission of the Sacred Heart, is a National Historic Landmark.
- **State Insect:** The Monarch butterfly, known for its striking orange and black coloration, is the state insect.
- **Mount Borah:** The state's highest peak is 12,668 feet tall and a popular destination for climbers.

Illinois

- **Pullman Strike:** The nationwide railroad strike in 1894 began in Pullman, Illinois and influenced labor laws and practices.
- **State Tree:** The state tree is the White Oak, a species that can live for hundreds of years.
- **Shawnee National Forest:** This area in southern Illinois is known for its dramatic rock formations and rich biodiversity.
- **Windy City:** Chicago's nickname, "The Windy City," isn't just about weather—it also refers to the city's "windy" politicians.
- **Lincoln-Douglas Debates:** The 1858 debates between Abraham Lincoln and Stephen A. Douglas took place in Illinois and have historical significance.
- **Illinois State University:** Founded in 1857, this is the oldest public university in the state.
- **Jazz and Blues:** Chicago has a rich history in jazz and blues music, with many influential artists originating from the city.
- **State Animal:** The White-tailed Deer, a common sight throughout the state, is the state animal of Illinois.
- **State Insect:** The Monarch butterfly, known for its long migration and distinctive appearance, is the state insect.
- **Chicago River:** This river is dyed green every year in celebration of St. Patrick's Day.
- **Rock and Roll McDonald's:** This iconic fast food restaurant in Chicago is a beloved city landmark.
- **Prohibition and Al Capone:** The era of prohibition made Chicago a hotbed for gangsters like Al Capone.
- **Frank Lloyd Wright:** The famous architect lived and worked in Illinois, and many of his most famous designs are located in the state.
- **O'Hare Airport:** One of the busiest airports in the world, O'Hare, is located in Chicago.

- **Popcorn State:** Illinois is the largest producer of popcorn in the United States.
- **Chicago Symphony Orchestra:** One of the "Big Five" American orchestras, it's known for its brass section.
- **Art Institute of Chicago:** This museum houses one of the largest and oldest permanent collections in the U.S.
- **Galena:** This charming town in northern Illinois is known for its well-preserved 19th-century buildings.
- **Ronald Reagan:** The 40th U.S. President was born in Tampico, Illinois, and raised in Dixon.
- **Chicago Stockyards:** At one time, more meat was processed in Chicago than in any other place in the world.

Indiana

- **Limestone:** Indiana limestone has been used in many iconic American buildings, including the Empire State Building.
- **Famous Astronaut:** Gus Grissom, one of the original NASA Mercury Seven astronauts, was from Mitchell, Indiana.
- **Kissing Bridges:** Indiana's covered bridges are sometimes called "kissing bridges" because couples would steal a kiss under the cover of privacy they provided.
- **Steel Production:** Indiana is the top steel-producing state in the U.S., with the city of Gary playing a significant role.
- **State Pie:** Indiana's official state pie is the sugar cream pie, also known as Hoosier pie.
- **Indiana State Fair:** One of the largest state fairs in the U.S., the Indiana State Fair, attracts millions of visitors each year.
- **Monon Trail:** This is a popular rail-trail in Indiana that extends from Indianapolis to Westfield.
- **Vincennes:** Founded by French fur traders, Vincennes is the oldest continually inhabited European settlement in Indiana.
- **James Whitcomb Riley:** This famous poet, known as the "Hoosier Poet," was born in Greenfield, Indiana.
- **State Song:** The official state song, "On the Banks of the Wabash, Far Away," was adopted in 1913.
- **Sliced Bread:** The first automated bread slicer was used by the Taggart Baking Company in Indianapolis, revolutionizing the way bread was sold.
- **RV Capital:** Elkhart, Indiana, is known as the "RV Capital of the World," with a large portion of American RVs manufactured there.
- **Fort Wayne:** Indiana's second-largest city, Fort Wayne, is named after the American Revolutionary War statesman Anthony Wayne.
- **Dan Quayle:** The 44th Vice President of the United States, Dan Quayle, is from Indianapolis.

- **Brown County State Park:** The largest state park in Indiana, it's especially popular during the fall when the leaves change color.
- **Tippecanoe River:** This river is known for its exceptional clarity and is one of the best canoeing rivers in Indiana.
- **Eli Lilly:** One of the largest pharmaceutical companies in the world, Eli Lilly and Company, was founded in Indianapolis in 1876.
- **Hoosier National Forest:** This national forest spans over 200,000 acres and offers a variety of outdoor recreational opportunities.
- **State Insect:** The Say's Firefly, known for its bioluminescent light production, is the state insect.
- **Madam C.J. Walker:** Considered the first self-made female millionaire in America, Madam C.J. Walker made her fortune in Indianapolis.

Iowa

- **Iowa Jima:** This famous WWII photograph was shot by Iowan photographer, Joe Rosenthal.
- **Winnebago:** The Winnebago Industries, known for manufacturing motor homes, was founded in Forest City, Iowa.
- **Mamie Eisenhower:** The wife of President Dwight D. Eisenhower, Mamie, was born in Boone, Iowa.
- **American Gothic:** The house that served as the backdrop for Grant Wood's iconic painting is located in Eldon, Iowa.
- **Eagle Days:** During the winter, you can spot hundreds of bald eagles along the Mississippi River in Iowa.
- **Mormon Pioneer National Historic Trail:** This trail follows the 1,300-mile route that Mormon pioneers traveled from Nauvoo, Illinois, to Salt Lake City, Utah, passing through Iowa.
- **Iowa Writers' Workshop:** This prestigious writing program at the University of Iowa has produced numerous Pulitzer Prize winners.
- **Music Man Square:** Located in Mason City, this attraction is dedicated to Meredith Willson, composer of "The Music Man".
- **Bix Beiderbecke:** This influential jazz cornetist, pianist, and composer was born in Davenport, Iowa.
- **Okoboji:** This popular vacation destination in Iowa is known for its beautiful glacial lakes.
- **Tugfest:** This annual event is a tug-of-war across the Mississippi River between teams from LeClaire, Iowa, and Port Byron, Illinois.
- **National Czech & Slovak Museum & Library:** Located in Cedar Rapids, this museum is the leading U.S. institution celebrating Czech and Slovak culture.
- **Grotto of the Redemption:** Located in West Bend, it's considered the largest man-made grotto in the world and contains the largest collection of precious stones and gems found anywhere in one location.

- **State Rock:** The official state rock of Iowa is the geode, which is a round stone with a hollow cavity lined with crystals.
- **Maytag Blue Cheese:** The world-famous blue cheese is made on the Maytag Dairy Farms in Newton, Iowa.
- **National Balloon Classic:** Every year, Indianola hosts this hot air balloon competition and festival.
- **Des Moines Art Center:** This contemporary art museum houses an impressive collection, including works by Grant Wood, Edward Hopper, and Georgia O'Keeffe.
- **Villisca Axe Murder House:** The site of a gruesome unsolved murder in 1912, it's now a museum and haunted attraction.
- **State Bird:** The state bird of Iowa is the American Goldfinch, also known as the Eastern Goldfinch.
- **Jazz Festival:** The Bix Beiderbecke Memorial Jazz Festival in Davenport is one of the largest jazz festivals in the U.S.

Kansas

- **Longest Railroad Bridge:** The Rock Island Bridge in Kansas City is the second longest railroad bridge of its kind in the U.S.
- **Capitol Building:** The Kansas state capitol in Topeka features a stunning 304-step dome tour that showcases a panoramic view of the city.
- **Geodetic Center:** The Meades Ranch Triangulation Station in Kansas is the Geodetic Center of North America—the reference point for all land surveying in North America.
- **Garden of Eden:** A unique folk art installation in Lucas, Kansas features concrete sculptures created by Civil War veteran Samuel P. Dinsmoor.
- **Fort Larned:** This well-preserved fort on the Santa Fe Trail was an important post in the Indian Wars.
- **State Reptile:** The Ornate Box Turtle is the state reptile of Kansas and can live up to 30-40 years in the wild.
- **Fort Leavenworth:** The oldest active Army post west of the Mississippi River, founded in 1827.
- **Insect Fossils:** The Niobrara Chalk formation in Western Kansas has yielded many important insect fossils.
- **Smoky Hills:** This region is named for the smoky appearance of its hills when viewed from a distance.
- **Schlitterbahn:** The waterpark in Kansas City, Kansas, was once home to the Verrückt, the world's tallest waterslide.
- **State Amphibian:** The Barred Tiger Salamander, known for its striking stripes, is the state amphibian of Kansas.
- **Sprint Center:** This large, multi-use indoor arena in Kansas City is a hub for major concerts and sporting events.
- **Boot Hill:** Dodge City's famous cemetery, Boot Hill, is a popular tourist attraction with a recreated 19th century street scene.

- **Big Basin Prairie Preserve:** This preserve in Clark County, Kansas, is home to a sinkhole that's nearly a mile in circumference and over 100 feet deep.
- **Eisenhower Presidential Library:** Located in Abilene, it's the presidential library and museum of Dwight D. Eisenhower, the 34th President of the United States.
- **Gypsum Hills:** These stunning, rugged hills in south-central Kansas are known for their red hues and are also referred to as the Red Hills.
- **Kaw River:** Also known as the Kansas River, the Kaw River is a tributary of the Missouri River and is approximately 170 miles long.
- **Cimarron National Grassland:** This grassland, the largest parcel of public land in Kansas, is part of the National Forest system.
- **State Flower:** The sunflower is the state flower of Kansas and can be found growing wild throughout the state.
- **Bleeding Kansas:** The term used to describe the period of violence during the settling of the Kansas territory, it was a precursor to the American Civil War.

Kentucky

- **Harland Sanders Café:** The first-ever KFC is preserved as a museum in Corbin, Kentucky.
- **Cumberland Falls:** Sometimes called the "Niagara of the South," Cumberland Falls is one of the few places in the world where you can see a moonbow.
- **Coal House:** The Williamson Coal House, made entirely from coal, is located in Middlesboro, Kentucky.
- **Lake Cumberland:** One of the largest man-made bodies of water east of the Mississippi River, known as a houseboat capital of the world.
- **Thunder Over Louisville:** The largest annual fireworks display in North America kicks off the two-week-long Kentucky Derby Festival.
- **Louisville Slugger:** The famous baseball bat manufacturer, Louisville Slugger, is headquartered in Louisville, Kentucky.
- **State Dance:** The official state dance of Kentucky is clogging, a type of folk dance.
- **Creation Museum:** A controversial museum in Petersburg, Kentucky, presents a literal interpretation of the Genesis creation narrative.
- **Shaker Village:** The largest historic community of the Shakers, a religious sect, is located at Pleasant Hill, Kentucky.
- **Jefferson Davis:** The birthplace of the president of the Confederacy during the Civil War, Jefferson Davis, is in Fairview, Kentucky.
- **Kentucky Music Hall of Fame:** Located in Renfro Valley, this museum honors Kentuckians who have made a significant contribution to the music industry.
- **Toyota Manufacturing:** Toyota's largest vehicle manufacturing plant in the world is located in Georgetown, Kentucky.

- **World's Largest Baseball Bat:** Located outside the Louisville Slugger Museum, it's an exact-scale replica of Babe Ruth's 34-inch Louisville Slugger bat.
- **Patton Museum:** Fort Knox is home to the General George Patton Museum of Leadership, housing a collection of U.S. military vehicles.
- **State Wild Animal:** The gray squirrel is the official wild game animal of the state of Kentucky.
- **Black Mountain:** The highest point in Kentucky, Black Mountain, reaches an elevation of 4,145 feet.
- **Daniel Boone National Forest:** Named after the explorer, this national forest covers over 2 million acres of rugged terrain.
- **State Drink:** Declared in 2005, the official state drink of Kentucky is milk.
- **Keeneland Race Course:** A National Historic Landmark, Keeneland Race Course in Lexington is one of the most stately and respected horse racing tracks in the world.
- **Wigwam Village Inn #2:** One of the last remaining "wigwam" motels is located in Cave City, Kentucky.

Louisiana

- **Atchafalaya Basin:** The largest wetland and swamp in the United States.
- **Mardi Gras:** Famous pre-Lenten festival celebrated with parades and masquerade balls in New Orleans.
- **Cajun Music:** A blend of French and African music traditions, often featuring the accordion and fiddle.
- **Lake Pontchartrain:** One of the largest bodies of water in Louisiana, it's an estuary connected to the Gulf of Mexico.
- **Plantation Homes:** Many antebellum plantation homes, such as Oak Alley and Magnolia, are located in Louisiana.
- **St. Louis Cathedral:** The oldest continuously active Roman Catholic Cathedral in the United States, located in New Orleans.
- **Voodoo Culture:** New Orleans is known for its historic voodoo practices, largely attributed to its Haitian immigrant population.
- **Zydeco Music:** A genre of music that evolved in southwest Louisiana by French Creole speakers blends blues, dance music, and African rhythms.
- **Alligators:** The state reptile of Louisiana, alligators are abundant in the state's wetlands.
- **The Mississippi Delta:** This region of Louisiana has been influential in developing blues music.
- **Louisiana Shrimp Industry:** Louisiana supplies 30% of the nation's shrimp.
- **Caddo Lake:** The largest natural freshwater lake in the South, straddling the Louisiana and Texas border.
- **Natchitoches:** Founded in 1714, it's the oldest permanent settlement within the borders of the 1803 Louisiana Purchase.
- **Audubon Zoo:** Located in New Orleans, this zoo is one of the top-rated zoos in the United States.

- **Napoleonic Code:** Louisiana's civil law system is based on the French Napoleonic Code, differing from the common law systems in other U.S. states.
- **USS Kidd:** A historic Fletcher-class destroyer from WWII, now a museum in Baton Rouge.
- **Lafayette:** The fourth-largest city in Louisiana, it's known as the heart of Cajun Country.
- **Cajun French:** A variant of the French language spoken in the Acadiana region of Louisiana.
- **Po' Boy Sandwich:** A traditional Louisiana sandwich, typically of fried seafood or roast beef on a baguette.
- **Chalmette Battlefield:** The site of the 1815 Battle of New Orleans, the last major battle of the War of 1812.

Maine

- **Moxie:** Moxie, one of the first mass-produced soft drinks in the U.S., is the official soft drink of Maine.
- **Puffins:** Maine is the only state in the U.S. where Atlantic puffins breed.
- **Tourmaline:** Maine is known for its high-quality tourmaline gemstones, and is the official state mineral.
- **International Appalachian Trail:** This trail extends from Maine's Mount Katahdin to Newfoundland in Canada.
- **Sailing:** Maine's extensive coastline and maritime history make it a great destination for sailing.
- **Penobscot River:** Maine's longest river, it's known for its recreational and fishing opportunities.
- **Snowfall:** Maine is one of the snowiest states in the U.S., with Caribou, Maine often recording some of the highest snowfall totals.
- **Passamaquoddy Bay:** Known for its extreme tidal range, with tides reaching up to 50 feet.
- **Baxter State Park:** This large wilderness area is home to Mount Katahdin, the highest mountain in Maine.
- **Museums:** Maine boasts numerous museums, including the Portland Museum of Art and the Maine Maritime Museum.
- **Forest Industry:** The forest products industry plays a significant role in Maine's economy.
- **Windjammers:** Historic sailing ships, known as windjammers, are a common sight off Maine's coast.
- **Sebago Lake:** The deepest and second-largest lake in Maine, it's a popular destination for boating and fishing.
- **Cumberland Fair:** One of the state's largest agricultural fairs, dating back to 1868.

- **Harpswell:** The town of Harpswell includes some of the state's most picturesque coastline, with 216 miles of coastline on Casco Bay.
- **Monhegan Island:** A small, rocky island 10 miles off the coast known for its artist colonies and natural beauty.
- **Bald Eagles:** After nearly becoming extinct in the state, bald eagles have made a significant comeback in Maine.
- **Wyeth Family:** The family of artists N.C., Andrew, and Jamie Wyeth have deep ties to Maine, and much of their work was inspired by the state.
- **Covered Bridges:** Maine is home to nine historic covered bridges.
- **Portland Head Light:** Located in Cape Elizabeth, it's the oldest lighthouse in the state and one of the most photographed in America.

Maryland

- **Largest Estuary:** The Chesapeake Bay is the largest estuary in the U.S, providing numerous economic and environmental benefits.
- **Rural Legacy Areas:** Maryland has the nation's largest Rural Legacy Areas aimed at preserving green spaces.
- **First Dental School:** The world's first dental school was established at the University of Maryland.
- **Cumberland Valley:** Maryland's Cumberland Valley is a vital migration corridor for birds of prey.
- **Inventive Residents:** Famous inventors such as Clarence Birdseye (quick-freezing process) and George D. Timanus (roller coaster) hailed from Maryland.
- **Smith Island Cake:** Maryland's state dessert, Smith Island Cake, features thin layers of cake and frosting.
- **Wire Suspension Bridge:** The first wire suspension bridge in the world was built in 1810 over Antietam Creek in Maryland.
- **Maryland's Flag:** Maryland's flag is the only state flag to be based on English heraldry (the coat of arms of noble family).
- **Smithsonian Affiliates:** Maryland has more Smithsonian Affiliates than any other state.
- **World's Largest Movable Bridge:** The Chesapeake Bay Bridge in Maryland is the world's largest movable bridge.
- **First Umbrella Factory:** The first umbrella factory in the U.S. was built in 1828 in Baltimore, Maryland.
- **Fort McHenry:** Fort McHenry in Baltimore is the birthplace of America's national anthem.
- **National Park for Performing Arts:** Wolf Trap National Park in Maryland is the only U.S. national park dedicated to presenting the performing arts.
- **US Naval Academy:** The U.S. Naval Academy, established in 1845, is located in Annapolis.

- **Women's Rights:** Maryland's Margaret Brent, in the 1600s, was the first woman in the American colonies to demand the right to vote.
- **Assateague Island:** Assateague Island in Maryland is famous for its wild horses that roam the beach.
- **Home of Harriet Tubman:** Maryland was the birthplace of Harriet Tubman, the famous abolitionist and "conductor" on the Underground Railroad.
- **Birthplace of Spiro T. Agnew:** Spiro T. Agnew, the 39th Vice President of the U.S., was born in Baltimore, Maryland.
- **Edgar Allan Poe:** The famous writer Edgar Allan Poe lived and died in Baltimore, Maryland.
- **Patuxent River Naval Air Station:** This facility is home to the U.S. Naval Test Pilot School.

Massachusetts

- **Freedom Trail:** The 2.5-mile long Freedom Trail in Boston is a historic route linking significant locations from the American Revolution.
- **Berkshires:** The Berkshire Mountains are a popular destination for outdoor activities and cultural events.
- **Fenway Park:** One of the oldest baseball parks in the U.S, Fenway Park is home to the Boston Red Sox.
- **American Literature:** Massachusetts was home to famed authors including Louisa May Alcott, Henry David Thoreau, and Edgar Allan Poe.
- **Witch City:** Salem, Massachusetts, is famously known as "Witch City" due to its history with witch trials.
- **Great Barrington:** Named the best small town in America by Smithsonian magazine in 2012, Great Barrington is located in the southwestern part of the state.
- **Plimoth Plantation:** This living museum in Plymouth replicates the original settlement of the Plymouth Colony.
- **Plymouth Rock:** This historic landmark is traditionally recognized as the disembarkation site of the Pilgrims.
- **State Reptile:** The official state reptile of Massachusetts is the Garter Snake.
- **World's Largest Paper Manufacturer:** The Crane Paper Company in Dalton, Massachusetts, has been the sole supplier of paper for U.S. currency since 1879.
- **First American Lighthouse:** The first American lighthouse was built in the Boston Harbor in 1716.
- **Lowell Textile Mills:** In the 19th century, Lowell became America's largest textile manufacturing center.
- **Nantucket Island:** This isolated island is known for its preserved late 18th-century architecture and beautiful beaches.

- **Economic Powerhouse:** Massachusetts is one of the top states in the U.S. for venture capital funding.
- **Worcester Diner Cars:** Worcester was once a major manufacturer of diner cars, leading to the term "Worcester Lunch Car" for a traditional diner.
- **Bean Town:** Boston, the state's capital, is often referred to as "Bean Town".
- **State Insect:** The ladybug is the official state insect of Massachusetts.
- **USS Constitution:** Also known as "Old Ironsides", this is the world's oldest commissioned naval vessel still afloat and can be visited in Boston.
- **Rockport's Motif No.1:** This fishing shack is reportedly the most-painted building in America.
- **Martha's Vineyard:** This affluent summer colony is known for being an occasional retreat for U.S. Presidents.

Michigan

- **Greenfield Village:** This outdoor living history museum in Dearborn showcases America's historical past.
- **First Soda Pop:** Vernor's Ginger Ale, first sold in 1866, is known as America's first soda pop and was created in Detroit.
- **Detroit River:** This river is the busiest waterway in the world in terms of volume.
- **State Tree:** The official state tree is the Eastern White Pine.
- **Record Breaking Snowfall:** The world's largest snowfall in a single day occurred in Michigan's Upper Peninsula in 1927.
- **Only Floating Post Office:** The J.W. Westcott II is the only floating post office in the U.S, serving freighters traveling on the Detroit River.
- **Detroit Symphony Orchestra:** One of America's oldest and most celebrated orchestras.
- **Frankenmuth:** Known as "Michigan's Little Bavaria", it's famous for its German roots and the world's largest Christmas store.
- **GM Renaissance Center:** This group of seven interconnected skyscrapers in Detroit serve as the global headquarters of General Motors.
- **Michigan's Dragon:** The state plans to build a 47-mile hiking and biking trail named "The Dragon" in Newaygo County.
- **Techno Music:** Detroit is known as the birthplace of Techno music, with pioneers like Juan Atkins and Derrick May hailing from the city.
- **Michigan State University:** Located in East Lansing, it's one of the largest universities in the U.S by enrollment.
- **Historic Windmill Island:** This tourist destination in Holland features a 251-year-old working Dutch windmill.
- **Pictured Rocks National Lakeshore:** Known for its stunning multicolored sandstone cliffs on Lake Superior.

- **Michigan International Speedway:** This venue hosts NASCAR races and is the fastest track in the sport.
- **Ottawa Indians:** Before European exploration, Michigan was populated by Algonquin people, including the Ottawa Indians.
- **Presidential Birthplace:** President Gerald Ford was born in Omaha, Nebraska, but was raised in Grand Rapids, Michigan.
- **State Fossil:** The official state fossil is the Mastodon, a prehistoric relative of the elephant.
- **Grand Hotel:** Located on Mackinac Island, the Grand Hotel's porch is reputed to be the world's longest.
- **Hockeytown:** Detroit is known as "Hockeytown" due to the success and popularity of the Detroit Red Wings.

Minnesota

- **Winter Carnival:** The Saint Paul Winter Carnival, a city-wide event featuring ice and snow sculptures, is the oldest and largest in the nation.
- **Garrison Keillor:** The humorist and host of "A Prairie Home Companion" hails from Anoka.
- **St. Anthony Falls:** The only waterfall on the Mississippi River is in downtown Minneapolis.
- **The Xcel Energy Center:** This Saint Paul arena is the home of the Minnesota Wild NHL team.
- **Skyway System:** Minneapolis has the world's most extensive skyway system, covering 11 miles and connecting 80 blocks downtown.
- **Fort Snelling:** Established in 1819, this fort played a central role in Minnesota's early history.
- **Northwest Angle:** This is the northernmost point in the lower 48 states, accessible by land only through Canada.
- **Mystery Cave:** The longest cave in Minnesota, it spans over 13 miles.
- **Mille Lacs Lake:** The second largest lake in the state is a premier walleye fishing location.
- **Guthrie Theater:** A centerpiece of Minnesota's vibrant theater scene, located on the Mississippi River in Minneapolis.
- **Largest Open Pit Iron Mine:** The Hull-Rust-Mahoning Mine in Hibbing is the largest open pit iron mine in the world.
- **Marjorie Kinnan Rawlings:** The Pulitzer-prize winning author of "The Yearling" was born in Washington D.C. but raised in Madison, Minnesota.
- **First Indoor Shopping Mall:** Southdale Center in Edina was the first fully enclosed, climate-controlled shopping mall in the U.S.
- **Minnesota Vikings:** The state's NFL team has appeared in four Super Bowls.

- **Grain Belt Beer:** This historic beer was once brewed in the largest brewery west of the Mississippi.
- **Largest Ball of Twine:** The largest ball of twine rolled by one man is located in Darwin.
- **Hormel Foods Corporation:** The food company known for products like SPAM is based in Austin, Minnesota.
- **Wanda Gag House:** The childhood home of the author and illustrator of "Millions of Cats," the oldest American picture book still in print.
- **Pillsbury Doughboy:** This iconic advertising character was created by the Minneapolis-based Pillsbury Company.
- **U.S. Hockey Hall of Fame:** Located in Eveleth, the "Cradle of American Hockey."

Mississippi

- **University of Mississippi:** This university, known as Ole Miss, was the first in the South to hire a female faculty member.
- **National Forests:** Mississippi has six national forests, more than any other Southern state.
- **Jim Henson:** The creator of the Muppets was born in Greenville, Mississippi.
- **Mississippi Freedom Trail:** This trail marks key sites of the Civil Rights Movement.
- **B.B. King Museum:** This museum in Indianola pays tribute to the legendary blues musician.
- **Mississippi River Museum:** This museum in Tunica provides a comprehensive look at the river's history and impact.
- **Delta Blues Museum:** Located in Clarksdale, this museum honors the history and culture of the Delta Blues.
- **King Cotton:** At one point, Mississippi produced more than half of America's cotton.
- **Vicksburg Bridge:** This cantilever bridge over the Mississippi River is an architectural marvel.
- **Canton Christmas Festival:** This annual event transforms Canton into a dazzling winter wonderland.
- **Grand Gulf Military Park:** One of the most well-preserved Civil War battlefields, located in Port Gibson.
- **Neshoba County Fair:** Known as Mississippi's Giant House Party, this event is the nation's largest campground fair.
- **Pascagoula:** Known as the Flagship City, Pascagoula is home to the state's largest employer, Ingalls Shipbuilding.
- **Mississippi Band of Choctaw Indians:** This is the only Federally recognized Native American tribe in the state.
- **Gulf Islands National Seashore:** This seashore is the largest protected area of the Gulf of Mexico.

- **Faulkner's Home:** The home of Nobel Prize-winning author William Faulkner, Rowan Oak, is in Oxford.
- **Pearl River:** This river forms most of the western boundary of the state.
- **National Civil Rights Conference:** This annual event takes place in Meridian, Mississippi.
- **Mound Bayou:** This town was an independent black community founded by former slaves in 1887.
- **Morgan Freeman:** The Oscar-winning actor co-owns the Ground Zero Blues Club in Clarksdale.

Missouri

- **Iced Tea:** This popular beverage was first served at the 1904 World's Fair in St. Louis.
- **Silver Dollar City:** This 1880s-themed amusement park in Branson attracts millions of visitors each year.
- **Caves:** Missouri is known as "The Cave State," with over 7,300 recorded caves.
- **Eads Bridge:** The first bridge to cross the Mississippi River, connecting St. Louis, Missouri, and East St. Louis, Illinois.
- **BBQ Sauce:** Kansas City style BBQ sauce, a thick, sweet, and tangy sauce, was born in Missouri.
- **Laura Ingalls Wilder:** The author of "Little House on the Prairie" lived in Mansfield, Missouri.
- **Bald Knobbers:** In the late 1800s, this vigilante group operated in the Ozark region of Missouri.
- **Lambert's Café:** Known as the "Home of Throwed Rolls," Lambert's is a beloved dining institution in Missouri.
- **Lake of the Ozarks:** With a shoreline longer than California's Pacific coast, it's a top destination for boating and fishing.
- **Mormonism:** In 1831, Joseph Smith declared Independence, Missouri, as the site of the future New Jerusalem.
- **Missouri Botanical Garden:** Founded in 1859, it's one of the oldest botanical institutions in the U.S.
- **Daniel Boone:** This American pioneer established a settlement called Boonesborough in Missouri.
- **Mules:** The official state animal is the mule, chosen for its role in Missouri's history of agriculture.
- **Joplin Tornado:** In 2011, a catastrophic EF5-rated tornado struck Joplin, causing significant damage and loss of life.
- **Wilson's Creek:** Site of the first major Civil War battle fought west of the Mississippi River.

- **Haunted Houses:** Kansas City is known for its high concentration of haunted houses.
- **World's Largest Fork:** A 35-foot tall fork resides in Springfield, Missouri, outside a food advertising agency.
- **Ha Ha Tonka State Park:** This park is home to a castle ruin, sinkholes, caves, and a large natural bridge.
- **Nelly:** This Grammy-winning rapper and singer was born and raised in St. Louis.
- **Maya Angelou:** The renowned poet and civil rights activist grew up in Stamps, Missouri.

Montana

- **St. Ignatius Mission:** Founded in 1854, its walls and ceilings have 58 original paintings by Brother Joseph Carignano.
- **Smokejumpers:** The largest training base for smokejumpers, firefighters who parachute into remote areas to combat wildfires, is located in Missoula.
- **Charles M. Russell:** A noted artist of the Old American West, he created more than 2,000 paintings of cowboys, Indians, and landscapes set in the Western United States and in Alberta, Canada.
- **Testicle Festival:** This annual event in Clinton, Montana features bull testicles as the main cuisine.
- **Bison Range:** The National Bison Range in Moiese is one of the oldest National Wildlife Refuges in the nation.
- **Malmstrom Air Force Base:** One of three U.S. Air Force Bases that maintains and operates the Minuteman III intercontinental ballistic missiles.
- **Ghost Towns:** Montana has more ghost towns than active towns, remnants of the mining era.
- **Elk Herds:** Montana's elk herds are some of the largest in the U.S.
- **Great Falls:** Known as the Electric City because of its numerous dams and power plants.
- **Earthquake Lake:** A lake created after an earthquake in 1959 caused a landslide blocking the Madison River.
- **Pictographs Cave:** A place to view rock paintings, some of which are 2,000 years old.
- **Mountain Goats:** The official state animal of Montana is the mountain goat, a species not found in any other state.
- **Crow Fair:** Often called the "Tipi Capital of the World," the Crow Fair begins every third Thursday in August and attracts more than 50,000 spectators.

- **Hutterite Colonies:** Montana has over 50 Hutterite colonies, more than any other state in the U.S.
- **Miles City Bucking Horse Sale:** Recognized as the world's premier bucking horse event.
- **Bozeman Trail:** An overland route connecting the gold rush territory of Montana to the Oregon Trail.
- **Bear Tooth Mountain:** This striking mountain is part of the Absaroka range and stands over 12,800 feet high.
- **Montana Yogo Sapphire:** The only North American gem to be included in the Crown Jewels of England.
- **Susan Gibson:** A Montana native, she wrote the song "Wide Open Spaces" which became a hit for the Dixie Chicks.
- **Fort Peck Dam:** The highest of six major dams along the Missouri River, located in the northeastern part of Montana.

Nebraska

- **Morrill Act:** This 1862 law providing land for agricultural colleges was named after Nebraska's Senator Justin Morrill.
- **National Museum of Roller Skating:** Located in Lincoln, it's the only museum in the world dedicated to roller skating.
- **Fort Robinson:** A former U.S. Army fort and now a state park, it's the site where famed Sioux Chief Crazy Horse died.
- **Nuclear Tests:** The country's first and only underground nuclear test was conducted in Nebraska's Panhandle.
- **Valentine National Wildlife Refuge:** A 72,000-acre refuge home to numerous bird species and the largest sand dunes in the U.S.
- **Willie O'Ree:** The first black player in the National Hockey League, he played for the minor-league Omaha Knights.
- **Nebraska National Forest:** The largest hand-planted forest in the United States, it spans over 140,000 acres.
- **Haymarket District:** Located in Lincoln, it's a vibrant neighborhood of shops, restaurants, and a weekly farmers' market.
- **Gerald Ford:** The 38th U.S. president was born Leslie Lynch King Jr. in Omaha.
- **The Overland Trail:** A stagecoach and wagon trail in the American West during the 19th century, much of which followed the Platte River.
- **Nebraska Furniture Mart:** Founded by Rose Blumkin in Omaha, it's the largest home furnishings store in North America.
- **Reuben Sandwich:** This famous grilled sandwich is claimed to have been invented at the Blackstone Hotel in Omaha.
- **Fred Astaire:** The legendary dancer and actor was born in Omaha in 1899.
- **Omaha Stockyards:** Once the world's largest livestock market, it was a key part of Nebraska's economy for over a century.

- **Ranching:** Nebraska has more acres of cattle ranching than any other state in the U.S.
- **Bighorn Sheep:** After being reintroduced, these majestic animals now roam freely in the Pine Ridge region of Nebraska.
- **Buffett's Giving Pledge:** Warren Buffett and Bill and Melinda Gates announced this commitment to donate their fortunes to charity in Omaha.
- **Johnny Carson:** The longtime "Tonight Show" host was born in Corning, Iowa, but raised in Norfolk, Nebraska.
- **Mayhew Cabin:** Nebraska's only site on the National Park Service's Underground Railroad Network to Freedom.
- **Brownville:** A historic river town, it's now a hub for the arts with a theatre, concerts, galleries, and bookstores.

Nevada

- **Nevada State Railroad Museum:** Located in Carson City, it showcases the state's railroad heritage with vintage train rides.
- **Valley of Fire:** Nevada's oldest state park, known for its vibrant red sandstone formations and ancient petroglyphs.
- **Wild Horse Populations:** Nevada is home to over half of America's free-roaming wild horse population.
- **Extraterrestrial Highway:** A section of State Route 375, close to Area 51, known for UFO sightings.
- **Legal Brothels:** Nevada is the only U.S. state where brothels are legal, though they are not allowed in Clark County (Las Vegas).
- **Levi Strauss:** The inventor of blue jeans, Strauss got his start selling goods during Nevada's 1850s silver rush.
- **Liberace Museum:** A museum dedicated to flamboyant pianist Liberace, showcasing his costumes, cars, and jewelry.
- **Mount Charleston:** Located near Las Vegas, it's a popular spot for skiing, hiking, and mountain biking.
- **Lovelock Cave:** A significant archaeological site, home to some of the oldest known examples of Native American basketry.
- **Winnemucca Petroglyphs:** The oldest known petroglyphs in North America, some dating back at least 14,800 years.
- **Largest Hotel:** The MGM Grand Las Vegas holds the title for the largest hotel in the U.S. by room count.
- **Biggest Little City in the World:** Reno's famous slogan, reflecting its small size but large array of amenities.
- **Las Vegas Chinatown:** One of the most notable Chinatowns in the U.S., known for its Pan-Asian businesses.
- **One Sound State:** Despite being the 7th largest state by land area, Nevada has only one area code: 702.
- **Nevada Test Site:** Location of over 900 nuclear tests conducted by the U.S. government between 1951 and 1992.

- **Las Vegas Marriage Licenses:** The city issues more than 80,000 marriage licenses annually, due to its easy, quick process.
- **Death Valley National Park:** Although mostly in California, this extreme desert landscape extends into Nevada.
- **Oldest Casino:** The Railroad Pass Hotel and Casino, opened in 1931, is the longest running casino in the U.S.
- **Black Rock Desert:** Known for its flat playa, one of the largest and flattest surfaces on Earth.
- **Cave Lake State Park:** A popular outdoor destination known for trout fishing, camping, and an annual ice fishing derby.

New Hampshire

- **Karner Blue Butterfly:** The state butterfly, a small blue species that is endangered across its range.
- **Free State Project:** An organized political migration to New Hampshire aiming to create a stronghold for libertarian ideals.
- **Balsams Wilderness:** At 7,700 acres, it's the largest ski resort by area on the East Coast.
- **Hampton Beach:** Known for its boardwalk, sandy beach, and oceanfront entertainment.
- **Concord Coaches:** Built in Concord, these horse-drawn vehicles were an essential mode of transport in the Old West.
- **Saint-Gaudens National Historical Park:** It preserves the home and studios of Augustus Saint-Gaudens, one of America's greatest sculptors.
- **Fall Foliage:** New Hampshire's autumn colors are famous, attracting leaf-peeping tourists every year.
- **Lobstering Legacy:** Despite being a small coastal state, New Hampshire has a robust lobster fishing industry.
- **Peterborough Town Library:** Founded in 1833, it's the oldest tax-supported public library in the U.S.
- **Jigsaw Puzzles:** Introduced in America by Stave Puzzles of Norwich, a leader in handcrafted wooden puzzles.
- **Moose Population:** New Hampshire is home to a significant moose population, particularly in the northern parts.
- **Saint Paul's School:** A prestigious boarding school, it's alma mater to many influential people.
- **Keene Pumpkin Festival:** This famous event once held the record for the most jack-o'-lanterns carved and lit in one place.
- **Craft Beer Industry:** New Hampshire's craft breweries have a substantial impact on the state's economy.
- **MacDowell Colony:** The first artist residency program in the U.S., located in Peterborough.

- **Tuckerman Ravine:** A popular destination for extreme skiing, located on Mount Washington.
- **Writers' Project:** Many notable authors have found inspiration in New Hampshire, including Robert Frost and J.D. Salinger.
- **Lake Sunapee:** Known for its crystal-clear water, it's a popular spot for boating and fishing.
- **The Flume Gorge:** A natural gorge extending 800 feet at the base of Mount Liberty in Franconia Notch State Park.
- **Live Free or Die:** The state motto, reflecting New Hampshire's commitment to individual liberty.

New Jersey

- **Diverse Ecosystems:** Ranging from Appalachian mountain forests to coastal marshlands and pine barrens.
- **Largest Cherry Blossom Collection:** Newark's Branch Brook Park has the largest collection of cherry blossom trees in the U.S.
- **Revolutionary War Sites:** New Jersey hosted more Revolutionary War battles than any other state.
- **Trenton Makes Bridge:** This iconic bridge over the Delaware River showcases Trenton's manufacturing heritage.
- **Birthplace of Sinatra:** Famed singer Frank Sinatra was born in Hoboken.
- **Morristown National Historical Park:** The winter encampments of George Washington's Continental Army are preserved here.
- **Lakota Wolf Preserve:** A unique sanctuary for wolves, located in Columbia.
- **Invention of the Light Bulb:** Thomas Edison invented the light bulb while working in Menlo Park.
- **Red Mill Museum:** A historic landmark in Clinton, captured in countless photographs and paintings.
- **Legendary Jersey Devil:** This mythical creature allegedly dwells in the Pine Barrens.
- **Land of Inventors:** Besides Edison, inventors like David Sarnoff and Albert Einstein lived in New Jersey.
- **Cranberry Production:** New Jersey is a leading producer of cranberries in the U.S.
- **Battle of Trenton:** A pivotal Revolutionary War battle, where Washington's forces defeated Hessian troops.
- **Great Falls Power Plant:** Alexander Hamilton chose this site to establish one of the nation's first planned industrial cities.
- **Garden State Parkway:** One of the world's busiest toll roads, stretching from Montvale to Cape May.

- **Elevated Railways:** The Hudson-Bergen Light Rail is a modern testament to New Jersey's innovative transportation history.
- **Campgaw Mountain:** A popular ski resort, offering winter fun close to the urban centers.
- **Skylands Region:** Renowned for its beautiful lakes, mountains, and forests in the northwest corner of the state.
- **Delaware Water Gap:** This impressive natural feature forms part of the border between New Jersey and Pennsylvania.
- **Invention of Color TV:** The first color television was invented at the RCA laboratories in Princeton.

New Mexico

- **Four Corners Monument:** The only place in the U.S. where four states intersect at one point.
- **Salinas Pueblo Missions:** Three historic mission ruins preserving a mix of Native American and Spanish cultures.
- **Gila Cliff Dwellings:** Cave dwellings from the late 1200s offer a glimpse into the lives of the Mogollon people.
- **International UFO Museum:** Located in Roswell, the museum explores the 1947 Roswell Incident and other UFO phenomena.
- **Cumbres & Toltec Scenic Railroad:** A historic narrow-gauge steam train offering scenic tours.
- **Santa Fe Trail:** A 19th-century transportation route connecting Missouri and Santa Fe.
- **Spanish Influence:** The oldest continuously used public building in the U.S., the Palace of the Governors, showcases Spanish colonial architecture.
- **Aztec Ruins:** Despite the name, these ruins were actually home to ancestral Puebloans, not the Aztecs.
- **Luminarias Tradition:** Each Christmas Eve, New Mexicans line their walkways, walls, and churches with luminarias, or farolitos.
- **Wild Spirit Wolf Sanctuary:** A sanctuary in Ramah that rescues and provides lifetime homes for wolves and wolf-dogs.
- **Trinity Site:** The location of the world's first atomic bomb detonation in 1945.
- **Kit Carson Home:** The Taos home of this famed frontiersman is now a museum.
- **Rattlesnake Museum:** Albuquerque's American International Rattlesnake Museum is a unique and interesting tourist attraction.
- **Navajo Nation:** The largest Native American jurisdiction within the United States is located in New Mexico.

- **Rio Grande Gorge:** A geological feature in Taos County, where the Rio Grande follows a tectonic chasm.
- **Acoma Pueblo:** Also known as Sky City, it's one of the oldest continually inhabited settlements in the U.S.
- **Wheeler Peak:** The highest point in New Mexico, at 13,167 feet above sea level.
- **Canyon Road, Santa Fe:** Home to over a hundred art galleries and studios.
- **Shiprock:** A striking volcanic rock formation located in Navajo Nation.
- **St. Francis Cathedral:** A beautiful example of Romanesque Revival style architecture in the heart of Santa Fe.

New York

- **American Museum of Natural History:** One of the world's preeminent scientific and cultural institutions.
- **Lake Placid:** Hosted the Winter Olympics twice, in 1932 and 1980.
- **Rockefeller Center:** A complex of 19 commercial buildings, known for its annual Christmas tree lighting.
- **Syracuse University:** Known for the Carrier Dome, the largest college campus domed stadium.
- **Madison Square Garden:** One of the world's most famous sports and entertainment venues.
- **Chautauqua Institution:** A unique summer center for arts, education, and religion.
- **Buffalo Wings:** The popular appetizer was first created in Buffalo in 1964.
- **Catskill Mountains:** Famous as the setting of Washington Irving's "Rip Van Winkle."
- **Saratoga Race Course:** One of the oldest horse racing tracks in the U.S., opened in 1863.
- **Long Island Iced Tea:** This potent mixed drink was created in Long Island in the 1970s.
- **Fort Ticonderoga:** A large 18th-century fort with significant history in the French and Indian War and the American Revolutionary War.
- **The Hamptons:** A summer destination for affluent New York City residents, with beautiful beaches and high-end amenities.
- **Harlem Renaissance:** A cultural, social, and artistic explosion centered in Harlem in the 1920s.
- **New York Cheesecake:** A style of cheesecake known for its rich and smooth texture.
- **Columbia University:** An Ivy League university located in Manhattan, founded in 1754.

- **Carnegie Hall:** A prestigious concert venue in Midtown Manhattan, known for its beauty, history, and acoustics.
- **Apollo Theater:** A noted venue for African-American performers, located in Harlem.
- **Corning Museum of Glass:** The world's largest glass museum, located in Corning.
- **Roosevelt Island Tramway:** Offering scenic views, it's one of the few aerial commuter trams in the U.S.
- **Woodstock:** The famous 1969 music festival actually took place in Bethel, not Woodstock.

North Carolina

- **Nantahala National Forest:** The largest of NC's four national forests, known for its whitewater rafting.
- **The Lost Colony:** The first English settlement in the New World mysteriously vanished and remains a mystery.
- **Mount Mitchell:** The highest peak east of the Mississippi River, located in the Black Mountain range.
- **Carolina Shag Dance:** The Shag is the official state dance, popular in coastal Carolina beach music clubs.
- **Bank of America Corporate Center:** The tallest building in both Carolinas, located in Charlotte.
- **Thomas Wolfe's "Old Kentucky Home":** The setting for the author's most famous novel, "Look Homeward, Angel."
- **NC Zoo:** The world's largest natural habitat zoo, located in Asheboro.
- **USS North Carolina:** A WWII battleship turned museum, docked in Wilmington.
- **Chimney Rock State Park:** Known for its 315-foot granite monolith, providing 75-mile views of Hickory Nut Gorge.
- **Crystal Coast:** This 85-mile stretch of coastline is known for its pristine waters and abundant marine life.
- **Emerald Isle:** A popular beach destination, it's named for the lush, green maritime forest that once covered the area.
- **Fontana Dam:** The tallest dam in the eastern U.S., created to produce hydroelectric power during WWII.
- **Blowing Rock:** A cliff overhanging Johns River Gorge, known for the wind that blows upwards from the rock.
- **Maggie Valley:** Home to Cataloochee Ski Area, one of the oldest ski areas in the U.S.
- **Wilmington's Historic District:** One of the largest historic districts in the U.S., spanning over 230 blocks.

- **The Biltmore's Winery:** The most visited winery in the U.S., located in Asheville.
- **Jockey's Ridge State Park:** Home to the tallest living sand dune on the Atlantic coast.
- **Fort Bragg:** The world's largest military installation in terms of population, home to the U.S. Army's XVIII Airborne Corps.
- **Richard Petty:** Known as the "King of NASCAR," he was born and still lives in Level Cross.
- **The Outer Banks:** A 200-mile string of barrier islands, known for its beaches and historic sites.

North Dakota

- **Turtle Mountain:** Home to the Turtle Mountain Band of Chippewa Indians and a beautiful mountain range.
- **Hjemkomst Center:** This Moorhead museum hosts a replica Viking ship that sailed to Norway.
- **Pembina Gorge:** Offers beautiful year-round outdoor activities, from kayaking to snowmobiling.
- **Medora Musical:** A popular summer musical held in the Burning Hills Amphitheatre.
- **Devils Lake:** The largest natural body of water in North Dakota, offering great fishing and outdoor activities.
- **Lake Metigoshe State Park:** Nestled in the Turtle Mountains, known for its natural and recreational offerings.
- **World's Largest Buffalo:** A 26-foot tall sculpture located in Jamestown.
- **Stave Churches:** Replica Norwegian Stave churches can be found in Minot and Fargo.
- **Dinosaurs' Playground:** Fossils from the late Cretaceous Period were discovered in the Hell Creek Formation.
- **Geographical Marvel:** The state's diverse geography ranges from the Red River Valley to the Badlands.
- **Bismarck's Art Alley:** A vibrant display of street art in the state capital's downtown.
- **Norwegian Festival:** Norsk Hostfest, the largest Scandinavian festival in North America, takes place in Minot.
- **Wind Energy:** North Dakota is a national leader in wind energy production.
- **Bully Pulpit Golf Course:** Located in Medora, offers stunning views of the Badlands.
- **Fargo Air Museum:** Showcases aviation history with vintage and modern aircraft.

- **McClusky Canal:** The longest federally constructed water conveyance system in the U.S.
- **Knife River Indian Villages:** Historic site that preserves Northern Plains Indians habitation sites.
- **Fort Union Trading Post:** A well-preserved 19th-century fur trading post on the Missouri River.
- **Wild Horses:** Theodore Roosevelt National Park is home to free-roaming wild horses.
- **Paul Broste Rock Museum:** Showcases rocks, minerals, and fossils from around the world.

Ohio

- **Hopewell Culture:** Hopewell Culture National Historical Park preserves the earthworks of the prehistoric Native American culture.
- **Put-in-Bay:** This village on South Bass Island is a popular summer tourist destination.
- **American Greetings:** The world's largest publicly traded greeting card company is headquartered in Cleveland.
- **Ohio River Scenic Byway:** A designated National Scenic Byway, it offers stunning river views.
- **Youngstown:** Once a major steel producer, Youngstown experienced a dramatic decline in the industry in the 1970s.
- **Cleveland Museum of Art:** It's renowned for its extensive collection and free admission.
- **Buckeye Football:** The Ohio State University Buckeyes are a top college football team with numerous national titles.
- **Dayton Aviation Heritage:** A National Historical Park in Dayton commemorating three significant American figures in aviation history.
- **Famous Musicians:** Artists like Dean Martin, The Isley Brothers, and John Legend hail from Ohio.
- **Johnny Appleseed:** John Chapman, also known as Johnny Appleseed, planted apple orchards across Ohio.
- **Akron Rubber Industry:** Akron was once known as the "Rubber Capital of the World".
- **Cleveland Orchestra:** Considered one of the "Big Five" American orchestras, known for its excellence.
- **Oberlin College:** The first college in America to admit women and African-American students.
- **Great Serpent Mound:** A prehistoric effigy mound, representing a serpent swallowing an egg.
- **Thomas Edison:** The great inventor was born in Milan, Ohio.

- **Horseshoe Crab:** The Ohio State fossil is the Isotelus, a type of ancient horseshoe crab.
- **German Village:** A historic neighborhood in Columbus, Ohio showcasing the city's German heritage.
- **Cincinnati Chili:** A unique culinary tradition of serving chili over spaghetti.
- **Mammoth Cheese:** The largest cheese wheel ever made was displayed in Ohio during the 1964 World's Fair.
- **William McKinley Library:** The 25th U.S. President's presidential library is located in Niles, Ohio.

Oklahoma

- **Wichita Mountains:** An ancient mountain range in southwestern Oklahoma, known for its wildlife refuge.
- **Green Corn Rebellion:** A 1917 uprising of tenant farmers against World War I.
- **Weather Variations:** Oklahoma has one of the most varied climates in the U.S., with extreme weather events common.
- **Washita Battlefield:** The site of a major battle during the Indian Wars, now a National Historic Site.
- **Scissor-Tailed Flycatcher:** The state bird of Oklahoma, known for its long forked tail.
- **Stockyards City:** A historic livestock market in Oklahoma City, one of the largest in the world.
- **Sequoyah's Cabin:** This state park preserves the cabin of Sequoyah, who created the Cherokee syllabary.
- **Bradley's Corner Store:** Built in 1890, it's the oldest general store still in operation in Oklahoma.
- **The Pioneer Woman:** Food Network star Ree Drummond runs her Mercantile store in Pawhuska.
- **Oklahoma State University:** One of the nation's top public research universities, located in Stillwater.
- **Survivor Tree:** A 90+ year old American elm in OKC that survived the 1995 bombing.
- **Quartz Mountain:** A popular hiking and rock climbing destination in southwestern Oklahoma.
- **Bartlesville:** Home to Price Tower, the only realized skyscraper designed by Frank Lloyd Wright.
- **Philbrook Museum of Art:** A fine arts museum located in Tulsa, housed in an Italian Renaissance villa.
- **Guthrie:** The state's first capital, known for its impressive Victorian architecture.

- **Oklahoma Rose:** The state flower of Oklahoma, a hybrid tea rose.
- **Cain's Ballroom:** A historic music venue in Tulsa, known as the "Carnegie Hall of Western Swing".
- **Golden Driller:** A 75-foot tall statue in Tulsa, symbolizing Oklahoma's oil history.
- **Turner Falls:** The state's largest waterfall at 77 feet, located in the Arbuckle Mountains.
- **Woody Guthrie:** The influential folk singer and songwriter was born in Okemah, Oklahoma.

Oregon

- **Dungeness Crab:** The Oregon Dungeness Crab is considered a delicacy and contributes significantly to the state's economy.
- **Astoria Column:** A 125-foot tower offering panoramic views of Astoria and the Columbia River.
- **Pittock Mansion:** A French Renaissance-style château in the West Hills of Portland.
- **Bend Beer:** Bend, Oregon, has one of the highest numbers of breweries per capita in the U.S.
- **Oregon Vortex:** A roadside attraction in Gold Hill, Oregon, known for its perceptual and visual anomalies.
- **Portland's Bridges:** Portland is nicknamed "Bridge City" due to its many distinct bridges.
- **Beverly Cleary:** The beloved children's author was born in McMinnville, Oregon.
- **Blue Star Donuts:** Another Portland-originated donut shop known for its gourmet donuts.
- **Goose Hollow:** A neighborhood in Portland known for its connection to fairy tales and folklore.
- **Witch's Castle:** An abandoned stone house in Portland's Forest Park rumored to be haunted.
- **Dee Wright Observatory:** An observation structure at the summit of McKenzie Pass in the Cascade Mountains.
- **Newberry Volcano:** A large shield volcano located 20 miles south of Bend, known for its beautiful lava flows.
- **University of Oregon:** Known for its research prowess and is the birthplace of Animal House.
- **Sasquatch Sightings:** Oregon is known for numerous reported sightings of Bigfoot, a cryptid hominid.
- **Hells Canyon:** The deepest river gorge in North America, located along the border of eastern Oregon.

- **Rose Festival:** Portland Rose Festival is a major civic celebration, held annually in June.
- **Shakespeare Festival:** The Oregon Shakespeare Festival in Ashland is one of the oldest and largest professional non-profit theaters in the U.S.
- **John Day Fossil Beds:** A national monument in Eastern Oregon, home to well-preserved layers of fossil plants and mammals.
- **End of the Oregon Trail:** Oregon City was the end destination for pioneers on the Oregon Trail.
- **Salem:** The capital of Oregon, is also known for its cherries.

Pennsylvania

- **Keystone State:** Pennsylvania's nickname, as it was the middle colony of the original 13 colonies.
- **First Computer:** The world's first general-purpose electronic computer, ENIAC, was created at the University of Pennsylvania.
- **Yuengling Brewery:** Located in Pottsville, it's the oldest operating brewing company in the U.S.
- **First Capital:** Philadelphia served as the U.S. capital from 1790 to 1800.
- **Oil Boom:** The world's first oil well was drilled in Titusville in 1859.
- **Electric City:** Scranton installed the first successful, continuously operating electrified streetcars in the U.S.
- **Pennsylvania Dutch Hex Signs:** Traditional folk art found on barns mainly in Pennsylvania Dutch Country.
- **Centralia:** This ghost town has had a coal mine fire burning beneath it since 1962.
- **Quakers:** William Penn founded Pennsylvania as a safe haven for his fellow Quakers.
- **First Stock Exchange:** The Philadelphia Stock Exchange, founded in 1790, was the first in America.
- **Mushroom Capital:** Kennett Square, PA, produces over a million pounds of mushrooms a week.
- **Pencil Sharpener Museum:** Located in Logan Mills, it's home to the world's largest collection of pencil sharpeners.
- **Fall Foliage:** Pennsylvania has a longer and more varied fall foliage season than any other state in the U.S.
- **Gifford Pinchot State Park:** Offers outdoor recreation on 2,338 acres of farm fields and forests in southern York County.
- **Ring Bologna:** A Pennsylvania Dutch specialty, popular in the southeast part of the state.

- **Longwood Gardens:** One of the premier botanical gardens in the U.S., located in Kennett Square.
- **Crayola Crayons:** Crayola's headquarters and main crayon factory are in Easton.
- **Chocolatetown:** Hershey is not only home to Hershey's chocolate but also the popular amusement park Hersheypark.
- **Christmas City:** Bethlehem is well-known for its annual Christkindlmarkt, a top holiday market.
- **Penn State:** One of the largest universities in the U.S., located in State College.

Rhode Island

- **Pawtucket:** The fourth largest city in the state, home to the iconic Slater Mill – the birthplace of America's Industrial Revolution.
- **Newport Jazz Festival:** The first annual jazz festival in America, established in 1954.
- **Providence Art Club:** One of the first art clubs in America to admit women on an equal basis with men.
- **Hasbro:** The multinational toy and board game company is headquartered in Pawtucket.
- **RISD Museum:** Associated with the Rhode Island School of Design, it's one of the leading art schools in the U.S.
- **Del's Lemonade:** A frozen lemonade that's a Rhode Island summertime staple.
- **Bristol's Fourth of July Parade:** The oldest continuous Fourth of July celebration in the U.S.
- **Ocean State:** Rhode Island's nickname, due to its multiple bays and inlets.
- **Trinity Repertory Company:** A premier regional theater located in Providence.
- **Rhode Island Greening Apple:** A variety of apple originating in Rhode Island in the 17th century.
- **Cabbage Night:** Rhode Island's name for the night before Halloween, traditionally involving mischief and pranks.
- **Quahogs:** A type of large clam, they're a culinary staple in Rhode Island.
- **Narragansett Beer:** A local brewery with a rich history dating back to 1888.
- **Rhode Island School of Design:** One of the world's best schools for art and design.
- **Jamestown Verrazzano Bridge:** A mile-long bridge crossing Narragansett Bay.

- **Portsmouth Abbey School:** A prestigious boarding school run by Benedictine monks.
- **Napatree Point:** A wildlife preserve in Westerly offering pristine beaches and birdwatching.
- **Providence Public Library:** The state's first public library and the third oldest in the U.S.
- **Easton's Beach:** Also known as "First Beach," it's the largest public ocean surf beach in Newport.
- **John Hay Library:** This Brown University library is home to a broad collection of rare books and manuscripts.

South Carolina

- **Angel Oak Tree:** An estimated 400-500 years old tree, believed to be one of the oldest living things in the U.S.
- **The H.L. Hunley:** The world's first successful combat submarine, used by the Confederacy during the Civil War.
- **Parris Island:** A key training site for the U.S. Marine Corps.
- **Carolina Marsh Tacky:** A rare breed of horse developed in South Carolina.
- **Riverbanks Zoo:** Located in Columbia, it's one of the top zoos in the U.S.
- **Table Rock State Park:** Named for a distinctive geological feature, it offers extensive hiking and camping opportunities.
- **Brookgreen Gardens:** A sculpture garden and wildlife preserve located just south of Murrells Inlet.
- **James F. Byrnes:** A South Carolinian who served in all three branches of the U.S. government.
- **The Citadel:** A military college in Charleston that dates back to 1842.
- **South Carolina BBQ:** Known for its mustard-based barbecue sauce, a regional specialty.
- **Lake Murray:** A man-made reservoir known for its fishing and boating opportunities.
- **USC Cocky's Reading Express:** A literacy outreach program of the University of South Carolina.
- **Sea Pines Forest Preserve:** A nature preserve on Hilton Head Island, home to a 4000-year-old Indian Shell Ring.
- **Kiawah Island:** A barrier island known for its golf resorts and wildlife.
- **South of the Border:** A roadside attraction with a Mexican theme, located along Interstate 95.
- **Drayton Hall:** The oldest preserved plantation house in America still open to the public.

- **Ninety Six National Historic Site:** An important site during the Southern Campaign of the American Revolution.
- **Sullivan's Island:** The entry point for about 40% of the enslaved Africans brought to British North America.
- **Middleton Place:** A plantation in Dorchester County, home to America's oldest landscaped gardens.
- **Duke's Mayonnaise:** A popular southern brand that originated in Greenville, South Carolina.

South Dakota

- **Dinosaur Park:** A free park in Rapid City, featuring seven dinosaur sculptures.
- **Ring-necked Pheasant:** This colorful bird is the state bird of South Dakota and a popular game bird.
- **Lewis and Clark Expedition:** The expedition travelled through what is now South Dakota in 1804 and 1806.
- **Belle Fourche:** Geographically recognized as the center of the United States.
- **Wounded Knee Massacre:** A tragic event in 1890 where hundreds of Lakota Sioux were killed by U.S. troops.
- **Sica Hollow State Park:** A place of Native American legends and considered sacred by many tribal communities.
- **South Dakota Air and Space Museum:** Located at Ellsworth Air Force Base, it showcases aviation warfare armaments.
- **SDSU Ice Cream:** South Dakota State University has been making its own ice cream since 1979.
- **1880 Town:** A real place that's been turned into a historical attraction with preserved buildings from the 1880-1920 era.
- **Spearfish Canyon:** A scenic byway known for its beauty and for the color-changing leaves in autumn.
- **Akta Lakota Museum:** Located in Chamberlain, it preserves the stories of the Northern Plains Indian Tribes.
- **Mitchell Prehistoric Indian Village:** An archaeological site where you can see a reconstructed lodge of the ancient agricultural people.
- **Storybook Island:** An admission-free children's theme park in Rapid City.
- **Great Plains Zoo:** Located in Sioux Falls, it houses over 1,000 animals from around the world.
- **Petrified Wood Park:** A park in Lemmon constructed from petrified wood, fossils, and stone.

- **Ingalls Homestead:** The original homestead of the Ingalls family, where visitors can experience prairie life.
- **Old Courthouse Museum:** An 1800s quartzite building in Sioux Falls that provides a glimpse into the area's past.
- **Dakota Wind Cave:** A sacred site of the Lakota people located in the Black Hills.
- **Woonsocket:** Known as the "Town with the Beautiful Lake", it is the geographical center of South Dakota.
- **Sioux Indian Museum:** Located in Rapid City, it displays the arts and crafts of the local Sioux tribes.

Tennessee

- **Oak Ridge National Laboratory:** The largest multi-disciplinary laboratory in the Department of Energy system.
- **The Peabody Ducks:** A flock of ducks live on the roof of the Peabody Hotel in Memphis and march to the lobby fountain daily.
- **Cherokee National Forest:** A large National Forest created on June 14, 1920 and located in the Southern Appalachian Mountains.
- **Bicentennial Mall State Park:** A 19-acre park in Nashville designed to complement the Tennessee Capitol Building.
- **Tennessee Titans:** The professional football team based in Nashville.
- **Rocky Top:** One of Tennessee's state songs and an anthem for the University of Tennessee.
- **Beale Street:** A historic street in Memphis known for blues clubs and BBQ joints.
- **Cumberland Plateau:** The southern part of the Appalachian Plateau in the Appalachian Mountains of the US, it's the largest remaining forested plateau in the continental United States.
- **Memphis Grizzlies:** The professional basketball team based in Memphis.
- **East Tennessee State University:** The state's oldest institution of higher education, located in Johnson City.
- **Lost Sea Adventure:** Located in Sweetwater, it's America's largest underground lake.
- **Cades Cove:** A broad, verdant valley surrounded by mountains, it's one of the most popular destinations in the Great Smokies.
- **The Ryman Auditorium:** Known as the "Mother Church of Country Music", the Ryman is a Nashville icon.
- **Fall Creek Falls State Park:** Tennessee's largest and most visited state park.

- **Tennessee Aquarium:** Located in Chattanooga, it's the largest freshwater aquarium in the world.
- **Lookout Mountain Incline Railway:** Known as "America's Most Amazing Mile", the railway is the world's steepest passenger railway.
- **Battle of Shiloh:** A significant Civil War battle took place in Shiloh in 1862.
- **Biscuits and Gravy:** This hearty Southern breakfast dish is popular throughout Tennessee.
- **Memphis in May:** An annual month-long festival featuring the World Championship Barbecue Cooking Contest.
- **Casey Jones Village:** A family destination in Jackson, dedicated to the legendary railroad engineer.

Texas

- **Houston Livestock Show and Rodeo:** The world's largest livestock show and rodeo event.
- **Willie Nelson:** The iconic country musician hails from Abbott, Texas.
- **Six Flags Over Texas:** The amusement park's name refers to the six countries that have governed Texas.
- **LBJ Ranch:** The "Texas White House" of President Lyndon B. Johnson.
- **Spindletop:** The oil field that led to the Texas Oil Boom, changing the economy of the US.
- **Beyoncé:** The internationally renowned singer was born and raised in Houston.
- **Enchanted Rock:** The largest pink granite monadnock in the United States.
- **Texas Rangers:** The oldest law enforcement agency in North America with statewide jurisdiction.
- **Brazos River:** The longest river in Texas, spanning 840 miles.
- **Padre Island National Seashore:** The world's longest undeveloped barrier island.
- **San Antonio River Walk:** A city park and network of walkways along the banks of the San Antonio River.
- **Chili:** The official state dish of Texas.
- **Selena Quintanilla-Pérez:** The "Queen of Tejano Music" was from Lake Jackson, Texas.
- **Fort Worth Stockyards:** A historic district that played a crucial role in the cattle drives.
- **The Texas Chain Saw Massacre:** The classic horror movie was filmed in Round Rock, Texas.
- **Moody Gardens:** An educational tourist destination, with a golf course and hotel in Galveston, Texas.

- **Buddy Holly:** The rock and roll pioneer was born in Lubbock, Texas.
- **Schlitterbahn:** The original waterpark and resort in New Braunfels, Texas.
- **Largest State in Contiguous US:** Texas is the largest state in the contiguous United States.
- **Barbecue:** Texas is famous for its unique style of barbecue, particularly Texas-style brisket.

Utah

- **Temple Square:** A 10-acre complex owned by The Church of Jesus Christ of Latter-day Saints in the center of Salt Lake City.
- **Snowboarding:** The first ski resort to allow snowboarding was Brighton Ski Resort in Utah.
- **Sundance Film Festival:** The largest independent film festival in the United States, held annually in Park City.
- **Bingham Canyon Mine:** One of the largest man-made excavations in the world.
- **Goosenecks State Park:** The park overlooks a deep meander of the San Juan River.
- **Dark Sky Parks:** Utah has the highest concentration of International Dark Sky Parks in the world.
- **Ancestral Puebloans:** Ancient Native American cultures that existed in Utah.
- **State Emblem:** The beehive symbolizes thrift and industry.
- **Uinta Mountains:** They're the highest range in the contiguous United States running east to west.
- **This is the Place Monument:** Commemorates the end of the Mormon pioneers' journey west.
- **State Cooking Pot:** Utah's state cooking pot is the Dutch oven.
- **Monument Valley:** An iconic region of the Colorado Plateau characterized by a cluster of vast sandstone buttes.
- **Bald Eagle:** Every winter, thousands of bald eagles migrate to Utah.
- **State Fossil:** The Allosaurus, a large carnivorous dinosaur.
- **Utah State University:** Founded in 1888, it's a leading research university known for its programs in education, engineering, agriculture, and more.
- **Cleveland-Lloyd Dinosaur Quarry:** Contains the densest concentration of Jurassic dinosaur fossils ever found.
- **Utah Lake:** The state's largest freshwater lake.

- **The Utah War:** An armed confrontation between Mormon settlers in Utah Territory and the U.S. government in 1857-1858.
- **Topaz Internment Camp:** A site where Japanese-Americans were interned during World War II.
- **State Mineral:** Copper, which is mined extensively in the Bingham Canyon Mine.

Vermont

- **Red Clover:** Vermont's state flower.
- **Billboards:** Vermont is one of four states in the U.S. that prohibit billboards.
- **Vermont Yankee Nuclear Power Plant:** Operated from 1972 until 2014, when it was decommissioned.
- **St. Johnsbury Athenaeum:** A library and art gallery that has been designated a National Historic Landmark.
- **Burlington:** The largest city in Vermont, known for its vibrant arts scene and historic architecture.
- **Smugglers Notch State Park:** Named after the smugglers who used the area's caves to hide goods during the embargo of 1807.
- **State Gem:** Grossular garnet, a mineral typically brown to reddish-brown.
- **Lake Willoughby:** The lake is a glacial lake over 300 feet deep in some places.
- **Kingdom Trails:** A network of recreational trails located in the Northeast Kingdom of Vermont.
- **Killington Resort:** The largest ski area in the Eastern U.S.
- **American Folklore:** The state is associated with several well-known folk figures, including Ethan Allen and Champ, the Lake Champlain monster.
- **State Song:** "These Green Mountains," adopted in 2000.
- **Granite, Marble, and Slate:** The state is known for its granite, marble, and slate industries.
- **Robert Frost:** The famous poet lived in Ripton, Vermont.
- **Snowboarding:** The first snowboard was developed in Londonderry, Vermont.
- **Champ:** A lake monster said to live in Lake Champlain, it's Vermont's Loch Ness Monster.

- **Marsh-Billings-Rockefeller National Historical Park:** Tells the story of conservation history and the evolving nature of land stewardship in America.
- **Vermont's State Fruit:** The apple.
- **Middlebury College:** A top liberal arts college, founded in 1800.
- **Sandhill Crane:** This bird species returned to Vermont in 2003 after a 100-year absence.

Virginia

- **Luray Caverns:** The largest and most popular caverns in the eastern U.S.
- **Virginia Creeper Trail:** A 34-mile biking and hiking trail from Abingdon to the North Carolina border.
- **Chesapeake Bay Bridge-Tunnel:** A 23-mile engineering wonder that combines bridge and tunnel sections.
- **Pocahontas:** The famous Native American woman was born in Virginia.
- **Monticello:** Thomas Jefferson's iconic Charlottesville home.
- **Bristol:** The birthplace of country music.
- **Chincoteague Ponies:** Wild horses that live on the barrier islands of Chincoteague and Assateague.
- **Tobacco:** Virginia's top agricultural product and an important part of the state's history.
- **The Pentagon Memorial:** Dedicated to the 184 people who died in the Pentagon and on American Airlines Flight 77 during the 9/11 attacks.
- **Booker T. Washington National Monument:** The birthplace of the famed African-American educator.
- **Robert E. Lee:** The Confederate general lived in Arlington House, which is now a national memorial.
- **Yorktown:** The site of the last major battle of the American Revolutionary War.
- **George Washington and Jefferson National Forests:** Combined, they cover over 1.8 million acres of land.
- **U.S. Department of Defense:** Headquartered at the Pentagon in Arlington.
- **Cardinal:** The state bird of Virginia, known for its vibrant red color.
- **Colonial Parkway:** A 23-mile scenic parkway linking Virginia's historic triangle: Jamestown, Williamsburg, and Yorktown.

- **Great Falls Park:** Offers stunning views of the Potomac River's powerful rapids.
- **Virginia State University:** One of the top historically black colleges and universities (HBCUs) in the country.
- **The Homestead Resort:** One of America's oldest and most prestigious resorts.
- **James River:** The longest river in Virginia, providing habitat for the endangered Atlantic sturgeon.

Washington

- **Grunge Music:** Bands like Nirvana, Pearl Jam, and Soundgarden started in Seattle.
- **Tacoma Narrows Bridge:** Known for the dramatic 1940 collapse of its first version, due to aeroelastic flutter.
- **Columbia River:** The largest river in the Pacific Northwest region of North America, creating a natural border between Washington and Oregon.
- **Hanford Site:** The production site for the plutonium used in the first nuclear bomb and the Fat Man bomb.
- **Chihuly Garden and Glass:** A museum in Seattle showcasing the studio glass of Dale Chihuly.
- **Washington State University:** One of the oldest land-grant universities in the American West.
- **Washington State Ferry System:** The largest ferry system in the U.S.
- **Lake Chelan:** The third-deepest lake in the U.S., reaching depths of 1,486 feet.
- **Puyallup Fair:** One of the largest fairs in the world, attracting over a million visitors each year.
- **Experience Music Project Museum:** Founded by Microsoft co-founder Paul Allen, the museum is dedicated to contemporary popular culture.
- **Makah Whaling:** The Makah people are the only tribe in the U.S. legally allowed to hunt whales.
- **Palouse Falls:** The official waterfall of Washington State, standing at 198 feet tall.
- **Lilac City:** Nickname for Spokane, due to the flowers that have flourished since they were introduced to the area in the early 20th century.
- **Marmot Population:** Washington has the largest marmot population in the U.S.

- **Walla Walla:** Known for its sweet onions and growing wine industry.
- **Leavenworth:** A Bavarian-styled village in the Cascade Mountains, known for its Oktoberfest celebration.
- **Skagit Valley Tulip Festival:** The festival showcases millions of tulips each April.
- **Bellingham:** The northernmost city in the contiguous United States with a population of more than 50,000.
- **Salmon Migration:** The Columbia and Snake Rivers have some of the longest salmon migration routes in the world.
- **Forks:** The setting for Stephenie Meyer's Twilight series.

West Virginia

- **Camden Park:** One of the country's oldest amusement parks, established in 1903.
- **Summersville Lake:** The largest lake in the state, it's known as "The Little Bahamas of The East."
- **Charles Town Races:** A renowned venue for thoroughbred horse racing.
- **Blenko Glass Company:** Famous for its hand-blown glass since 1893.
- **Matewan Massacre:** The site of a 1920 battle between coal miners and coal company security guards.
- **Coal House:** A unique building in Williamson constructed entirely from coal.
- **Mystery Hole:** An unusual roadside attraction near Ansted that defies the laws of physics.
- **Tudor's Biscuit World:** A popular regional fast-food chain specializing in biscuits.
- **Hatfield-McCoy Trails:** One of the largest off-highway vehicle trail systems in the world.
- **Wheeling:** Known as the original state capital and the birthplace of West Virginia.
- **West Virginia Day:** The state holiday commemorates the admission of West Virginia to the Union on June 20, 1863.
- **Berkeley Springs:** A historic spa and art-filled town nestled in West Virginia's Eastern Panhandle.
- **Mountain Stage:** A live music radio show produced by West Virginia Public Broadcasting and distributed by NPR.
- **Oglebay Park:** A self-supporting public municipal park, the only one of its kind, located on the outskirts of Wheeling.
- **Elkins:** Known for the Augusta Heritage Center, a focus of traditional music, dance, craft, and folklore.

- **Jackson's Mill:** The boyhood home of Stonewall Jackson, one of the Confederacy's most successful generals during the American Civil War.
- **Helvetia:** A small Swiss settlement known for its quaint customs and cheese making traditions.
- **Coonskin Park:** A park and recreation area in Charleston, offering golf, swimming, and other outdoor activities.
- **West Virginia State Penitentiary:** A gothic-style prison where tours are offered, including the option to stay overnight.
- **Cathedral State Park:** An ancient hemlock forest of majestic proportions, it's one of the last living commemorations of the vast virgin hemlock forest which once covered the Appalachians.

Wisconsin

- **Olbrich Botanical Gardens:** Named one of the top ten most inspiring gardens in North America by Horticulture Magazine.
- **Milwaukee Public Market:** An indoor year-round market with a variety of high-quality artisan and ethnic products.
- **Hodag:** A mythical creature that serves as the mascot of Rhinelander.
- **Frank Lloyd Wright:** The renowned architect was born in Richland Center and designed several buildings in the state.
- **Apostle Islands:** Known for their scenic beauty and historic lighthouses, located in Lake Superior.
- **Wisconsin State Cow:** The dairy cow, symbolizing Wisconsin's significant dairy industry.
- **Milwaukee Brewers:** The state's Major League Baseball team.
- **Bay Beach Amusement Park:** One of the oldest amusement parks in the U.S., located in Green Bay.
- **Roth Cheese:** The first U.S. cheese to win the World Cheese Championship.
- **Cranberry Production:** Wisconsin is the leading producer of cranberries in the U.S.
- **Jazz in the Park:** A popular free outdoor music series in Milwaukee.
- **Lake Winnebago:** The largest inland lake in Wisconsin, it's a favorite among locals for fishing and boating.
- **Eagle River:** Known as the Snowmobile Capital of the World, it hosts the annual World Championship Snowmobile Derby.
- **Beloit International Film Festival:** This annual film event showcases over 100 independent films from around the world.
- **Badger State:** A nickname given to Wisconsin referencing lead miners of the 1820s and 1830s who burrowed into the hillsides for shelter, like badgers.
- **Lakes Galore:** Wisconsin is home to more than 15,000 lakes.

- **Sturgeon Spearing:** Lake Winnebago hosts the world's largest sturgeon spearing festival.
- **Fish Fry Tradition:** The Wisconsin fish fry is a cherished weekly ritual across the state.
- **Wisconsin State Dance:** The polka, a popular social dance in the state.
- **The Pabst Theater:** A historic landmark in Milwaukee, it's the fourth oldest operational theater in the U.S.

Wyoming

- **Continental Divide:** A part of this divide, which separates the waters flowing to the Atlantic and Pacific Oceans, runs through Wyoming.
- **Gillette:** Known as the "Energy Capital of the Nation" due to its vast resources of coal, oil, and methane gas.
- **Powder River Basin:** One of the largest coal producing areas in the U.S., located in northeastern Wyoming.
- **Sweetwater County:** The largest county in Wyoming, larger in size than six U.S. states.
- **Independence Rock:** A historic landmark on the Oregon Trail where pioneers inscribed their names.
- **University of Wyoming:** The state's only public four-year institution of higher learning.
- **Pronghorn Antelope:** Wyoming has the largest population of pronghorn in North America.
- **Jackson Hole:** Known for its world-class skiing, mountain climbing, and its rich cowboy history.
- **Ames Monument:** A large pyramid in Albany County, built to commemorate the Ames brothers who helped finance the Union Pacific Railroad.
- **Dinosaur Fossils:** Wyoming has been a rich source of dinosaur fossils; the first Triceratops was discovered here.
- **Wyoming State Fair:** An annual event since 1886, it celebrates Wyoming's agricultural heritage.
- **Wind Energy:** Wyoming is one of the top states for wind energy potential.
- **Laramie:** The city is home to the Wyoming Territorial Prison which once held notorious criminals like Butch Cassidy.
- **Grizzly Bears:** Wyoming's Yellowstone region is one of the few areas in the U.S. where grizzly bears can still be found.

- **National Elk Refuge:** Located in Jackson Hole, it's one of the largest elk preserves in the U.S.
- **Cowboy State:** Another nickname for Wyoming, a nod to its deep cowboy and rodeo culture.
- **Bison:** The state mammal of Wyoming, bison herds can be seen in Yellowstone National Park.
- **Sinks Canyon:** A unique geological feature where the Popo Agie River disappears into a cavern and reappears in a trout-filled pool.
- **Fort Laramie:** A significant 19th-century trading post and diplomatic site located at the confluence of the Laramie and the North Platte rivers.
- **Cheyenne:** The state's capital and largest city, known for its vibrant Western character.

Conclusion

And here we are, at the close of our second volume of "1000 Facts about The United States of America". As you complete these 1000 new facts, we hope you have savored the journey, marveling at the varied landscapes, historical milestones, and cultural idiosyncrasies of this incredible nation.

We have traversed vast plains and towering mountains, met the challenge of revolutions, and celebrated the joys of regional cuisines, sports, and community. The United States, in all its complexity, has unfolded before us, offering us new perspectives on a land of staggering diversity and incessant innovation.

This volume has taken you on an enlightening journey through the rich tapestry of America, from its most recognizable landmarks to the lesser-known corners where hidden gems lie. You have glimpsed the innovation of its cities, the serenity of its rural expanses, the triumphs, and the tribulations that define its narrative.

As we bid farewell to this volume, remember that our journey is not yet complete. An additional 1000 captivating facts await in the third and final volume of this series, ready to unveil the concluding chapters of our tale. The saga continues, and we hope you join us for the final part of this enriching journey.

As we leave the world of this volume, we extend our thanks for your companionship on this journey and invite you to continue exploring the depth and breadth of America's story. Onwards to the next chapter!

Daniel Scott